INTERNET
101

for the Fine Artist

with a special guide to

Selling Art on eBay

ArtNetwork

INTERNET 101 FOR THE FINE ARTIST, WITH A SPECIAL GUIDE TO SELLING ART ON EBAY

Copyright 2004 by Constance Smith and Susan F Greaves

Published by ArtNetwork, PO Box 1360, Nevada City, CA 95959-1360
800·383·0677   530·470·0862   530·470·0256 Fax
www.artmarketing.com   <info@artmarketing.com>

ArtNetwork was created in 1986 with the idea of teaching fine artists how to earn a living from their creations. In addition to publishing art marketing books and newsletters, ArtNetwork also has a myriad of mailing lists—which we use to market our products—available for rent. See the back of this book for details.

Susan F Greaves can be contacted at www.susanfgreaves.com or www.pitchfordart.com.

Smith, Constance, 1949

Internet 101 for the fine artist : with a special guide to
        selling art on ebay / by Constance Smith and
        Susan F Greaves. -- 1st ed. -- Nevada City, CA : ArtNetwork, 2004.
                p. ; cm.
                (101 series)
                Available in print and as a PDF file via e-mail from the publisher.
                Includes index.
                ISBN: 0-940899-95-7

                1. Art--Marketing. 2. Selling. 3. Internet marketing. 4. Internet.
                    I. Greaves, Susan   II. Title.

HF5415.1265 .S65 2004
658.8/72 --dc22   0401

DISCLAIMER: While the publisher and author have made every reasonable attempt to obtain accurate information and verify same, occasional address and telephone number changes are inevitable, as well as other discrepancies. We assume no liability for errors or omissions in editorial listings. Should you discover any changes, please write the publisher so that corrections may be made in future editions.

ISBN: 0-940899-95-7

TABLE OF CONTENTS

Chapter 6   Designing Your Website

Chapter 7   Making a Splash on the Web

Chapter 8   Search and You Shall Find

INTRODUCTION

In 1995 an onslaught of TV, radio and print media hype occurred, all introducing the World Wide Web. Previous to that, most people didn't know what this term was all about. The World Wide Web was coming of age. All this buzz got me interested. My entrepreneurial desires were piqued. I took a web design class. It made me realize the complexity of this new World Wide Web. Many companies were investing thousands of dollars in building their websites. Web-related professionals became the new hot item.

With all the TV glitz, followed by print media, the world was abuzz with the WWW. Investors brought out their checkbooks. Web businesses (even in the red) had their CEOs on the cover of *Time* magazine as "CEO of the year." Small-time investors, small-time inventors and small-time employees were made into millionaires practically overnight. This was the big boom time. People saw future fortunes and pursued them.

By 2000 the gold rush was over. Many companies fell prey to sites full of flaws; additionally, the people didn't arrive to buy. Selling something online took as much effort as selling something from a store. Investors learned that long-term planning should be the prime factor in determining their investment.

The world of art has, undoubtedly, been affected by the World Wide Web, albeit perhaps more slowly than other commodities. The real effect for the artworld will take place in 10 to 20 years. The Internet is a means for displaying your artwork—a new way to find potential clients. At present, the Internet is not only a mode of *introducing* art, but it is being used for selling art—not just prints but even $10,000-15,000 originals. People keep saying, "No one will buy art over the Internet." They have already been proven wrong.

Susan F Greaves has added an in-depth chapter about making sales on eBay. She sold art on eBay to the tune of $30,000 one year, and other artists earn even more. Follow her easy instructions and you, too, may make that amount.

My personal hope for the creative world (visual arts, poetry, literature) is that the Internet will enable those who might not otherwise have their voices heard. Perhaps then the artworld will not be so controlled by the critics, historians and gallery owners but more by popular demand. Perhaps the general public will become more educated about art, incorporating more art into their lives. Surely this would be a revolution.

Constance Smith

WHY THIS BOOK?

Knowledge empowers. Hopefully, this book will fill the gaps and correct the myths about art on the Internet.

For an artist, the web is a different marketing tool than for mass marketers. "How many hits does your site get a day?" is not as important a qustion for you as it is for amazon.com. The important thing for artists is to get the *right* hits, the *right* people to visit their site.

In writing this book, I wanted to create a user-friendly tool that would take artists, step-by-step, into a new mode of publicity, communication and promotion. I've tried to keep it simple.

For whom is this book written?

The business of marketing art has become more and more complex, more and more sophisticated. An artist must continue to become educated in the new ways of business, just like any other entrepreneur. This handbook teaches artists how the Internet can help their careers.

Internet 101 is designed for the total novice as well as the slightly experienced.

Artists who are serious about marketing their art must adapt to the ways of the Internet. Successful entrepreneurs not only adapt—they use a new tool to their advantage. That is what I hope you will learn to do as you progress through this book. The Internet is new for all of us, and we'll all have to make investments of time, equipment and energy. Let's make those investments worthwhile.

Fears, frustrations and preference for spending time creating art are reasons (but not good ones) that you may not learn to use the Internet to your advantage. Nevertheless, the Internet has become a fact of life. If your business doesn't have e-mail, you look prehistoric. If you don't have a web presence, people who use the web don't believe you're serious.

The Internet and change are synonymous. Keep updated on what's new by going back to your favorite bookmarked sites, subscribing to appropriate newsletters and searching out new information.

In Internet 101 you will learn:

➤ E-mail communication

➤ Creative tricks and shortcuts for using the Internet for research

➤ The advantages of having a home page on the web

➤ Basic design layouts for an artist's website

➤ Basic promotional techniques for attracting clients to your site

➤ Creative ideas to enable you to sell art online

Everything we do reflects who we are. In most areas of our lives, the clarity of our goal has a direct relationship to the success that we achieve with it. This book is intended to help you create a clear goal in the area of marketing your fine art, using the Internet as a tool.

HOW TO USE THIS BOOK

Treat this book like a workbook. Conquer chapters one at a time in order. Most of the knowledge builds on itself. Fill in the blanks. Talk the lingo. Make notes throughout the book. Use the Action Plan at the end of each chapter to create your online marketing plan.

Designed after our best-selling book *Art Marketing 101*, the chapters are simple to read, with plenty of space to jot down notes. Write all over the margins, as it will help you to remember ideas. The detailed Table of Contents and Index make it easy to find the exact topic for which you are looking.

Do not browbeat yourself. Do not study and work on the Internet if you are in a stressed, frustrated, irritated or bad mood. It could take you to the brink! If you see yourself getting frustrated by slow downloads, losing information, or being unable to find what you want, shut down the computer and go back later. It's not worth the loss of your energy.

There is an entire new language you will have to learn. When you see a new word in the text of this book and need a definition, look in Chapter 1, pages 13-15. No need to memorize these definitions. Soon they will simply become part of your business vocabulary.

The listings in the resource section (Chapter 7) should not be interpreted as an endorsement. No advertising was accepted for this book. Due to the transitory nature of so many dot-com companies, some of the addresses listed might have changed or gone out of business by the time this publication reaches you. If you know of such an occurrence, we would appreciate it if you e-mail any corrections to us at <info@artmarketing.com>. Please note "101 update" in the subject line of your e-mail.

If you have any topics you would like covered in future editions, or any questions about something covered here, please let us know at info@artmarketing.com.

Note: We have not listed websites with the "www" in front of them when they are within a list. We have added the ".com" ending and "www" when we use the name within a sentence. We've only included the unusual endings, such as .org, .edu, etc.

Have a blast—stay on track. Explore to your heart's content!

Chapter 1
Basics

A little history

Equipment

Lingo

Before every new form there is a period of chaos.

A LITTLE HISTORY

The Internet was developed in the late '60s for the military's use. This system assured that, providing the phone lines didn't collapse, people would be able to communicate with each other in the event of a catastrophe. Computers were large, expensive and difficult to use in those days.

Small personal computers were not developed until the mid-'70s. During this same period, what was first called ARPANET began to be called Internet, with links from the U.S. to Britain and Norway.

Realizing the potential for communication with all people via their personal computers, some savvy engineers in the '70s began to experiment, eventually coming up with this huge computer network called the World Wide Web, aka WWW. This WWW was invented in 1989 at CERN in Geneva, at the greatest European physics lab. Only after that did the Internet become popular outside universities and research centers.

In 1993, Marc Andressen, a 23-year-old student at the University of Illinois and founder of Netscape, invented Mosaic, the first browser able to visualize images in web documents. Soon, all kinds of businesses were interested in exploiting this new resource. Some say it was similar to the Gold Rush in California.

History continues today—with web music, live web broadcasts ("webcasts") and more.

EQUIPMENT

Whether or not you ultimately decide to expose your artwork on the Internet, as an entrepreneur you will need to know how to use a computer, receive and send e-mail and browse the web. You must become computer-literate to that degree—not a whiz-kid, but literate enough to know how to type and print out a letter, access the Internet, and send e-mail. Additionally, knowledge of graphic programs (for example, Photoshop) will save you tons of money during your fine art career. The more you know, the better off you will be.

You will need to invest in a variety of business machines that help you accomplish your business tasks. Start with the right tools and make your climb to success easier. If you don't wish to invest in these tools (or feel you can't), it will be a great hindrance and most likely will slow your progress considerably.

COMPUTERS

If you already own a computer, great. If you are unfamiliar with computers and don't know how to choose one, an introduction is in order. (Perhaps an introductory course at a local high school would be a good route to take.)

There are two computer systems available: PC (personal computers such as Compaq, IBM, Gateway) and Macintosh (Apple Corporation makes iMac and other such models). The two groups of computers recently have become a bit more compatible: Both now use a USB cable, and data and text can be interchanged between these two types of computers via a diskette, CD or the web.

Most creatively-oriented people (i.e., artists, designers, musicians) use the Macintosh system. Retail stores such as Computer Warehouse, CompUSA and others are offering iMacs at a very low price ($795+). We use the iMac for our entire publishing business: books, accounting, Internet, data entry and more. You can even use it to watch DVDs! iMacs come with an internal modem and Internet software to start you off.

Macs are more innovative, trendy, stylish; PCs are usually less expensive (with many clone models available) and usually have

DSL/Direct Service Line
Available in many locations nationwide, a DSL line connects you to the WWW over 100 times faster than the fastest modem. If you are a heavy user of the Internet, this is the way to go. If you are a heavy user of e-mail, it is not necessary to buy this service. It costs about $35 per month plus initial equipment fee of $100. For now, start with the basics; consider a DSL line for a future investment. You can always upgrade.

more software programs available. With the advent of Windows, both systems are very user-friendly.

Since this is not a computer course but an introduction to using the Internet, we will not deal with computer basics here.

MODEMS

A modem is a device that connects your telephone line to the WWW and transmits computer data. This machine can be an "external peripheral," although these days it is generally built directly into the computer. Modems come in different "speeds"— 28,000 to 56,000. If your computer doesn't have an internal modem, purchase the fastest external peripheral that's available. Software to run your new modem will come with it, which you must then install into your computer.

You can use your regular home telephone line for your Internet connection. Many phone companies offer to make your one-line system into a two-line system—one for your Internet connection, and one to answer the telephone calls. Phone your local telephone company for particulars in your area.

PRINTERS

Ultimately, if you have a computer, you will need a printer. Dot-matrix or ink-jet color printers are inexpensive these days. Most of the expense comes with the cost of ink cartridges. There are also laser printers. Many models come equipped wth fax, photocopier and computer printer all in one.

DIGITAL CAMERAS

Most digital cameras' output quality exceeds the needs of the web. If you have a digital camera and are a good photographer, this might be the most direct way to get your artwork onto the Internet. One online resource is www.digitalcameraresource.com.

SCANNERS

You will need to transfer your artwork into digital format to upload it onto the Internet. To do this, the artwork itself (if it is small) or a reproduction of it has to be "scanned." Professional scanners, such as the ones used by large pre-press service bureaus, offer the best quality of high-resolution output and color fidelity. Images scanned on smaller scanners usaully need some reworking with a photo imaging program such as PhotoShop to correct or adjust colors and contrast.

If you want to scan slides at home, you will have to invest in a slide scanner. You can scan photos on less expensive "flatbed" scanners. Some flatbed scanners also have an attachment to scan slides.

Service bureaus such as Kinkos (or your local copy house) can take a slide or print of your work and create a digital file for a nominal fee—usually about $5-10.

TIPS

➤ Have scans made to 300dpi (dots per inch) resolution. From this 300dpi scan, you will be able to create a 72dpi jpg for your website.

➤ You might need a CD drive on your computer in order to transfer these large scan files.

RESOURCE

Visual Horizons
180 Metro Park, Rochester, NY 14623 (800) 424 1011
www.storesmart.com <info@storesmart.com>
They scan slides and photoprints. Call or go online for prices and brochure.

LINGO

This glossary has been put in the first chapter so you can acquaint yourself with these terms right away. You can refer back to these pages when necessary. Soon you will remember all the definitions.

404 error - this page pops up when a link doesn't work online

Address book - stores all your e-mail addresses in specific categories within your e-mail software

Attachment - a file (or advertisement) that comes in an e-mail that you will need to download in order to open. It can be an image, text, music, etc.

Banner - an ad on a website, often containing the logo of the advertiser with a link to their site

BBS - an online bulletin board system; this allows users to hold discussions and make announcements that others can then read and respond to

BCC/Blind carbon copy - a way to send e-mail to several people at once without them seeing the addresses of the other recipients

Bit - the smallest unit of memory (a combo of binary and digit)

Bookmark - a way to save the address of a website with your browser program so that it is easy to retrieve later

Browser - a software program, such as Microsoft Internet Explorer or Netscape Navigator, that enables you to navigate the Internet and receive e-mail

Cache - a page you've opened on the Internet that is automatically stored in your computer

CGI/Common Gateway Interface - programming protocol for interactive sites that have guest books, order forms, etc.

Chat room - an area in an online service where several users can "talk" simultaneously and exchange messages

Cookie - data that are placed in your computer when you visit a site. This site can then trace your actions: what you buy, where you browse, etc. Many sites you visit on the WWW will deposit invisible "cookies" onto your computer allowing them to identify you when you return. Cookies can be invasive. To see how cookies work, visit www.privacy.net, a consumer-protection site. To learn how to view, manage and delete cookies, visit www.cookiecentral.com.

Dial-up connection - a connection to the Internet using a telephone line

Discussion group - an electronic message board that contains notes focusing on a specific topic

Domain - an Internet address or home page

Download - the process of receiving files from the web onto your computer

DPI - dots per inch. Your computer screen has a resolution of 72dpi.

E-mail - acronym for electronic mail, a method of communication via the Internet

Ezine - an online magazine

FAQ - Frequently Asked Questions; you'll find this on many sites so they don't have to answer the same questions over and over via e-mail.

Font - a typeface used in text layout

Forum - a discussion group online

FTP/File Transfer Protocol - a program that allows you to upload and download data onto the Internet

GIF - a graphic format for the Internet used mostly for items other than fine art

Hit - each time a visitor clicks on a new web page, it is counted as a hit

Home page - the first page of a website

Host - a company that gives you space online to store your website

HTML/Hyper Text Markup Language - the coding language used to create web pages for use on the Internet

HTTP/Hyper Text Transfer Protocol - the system of communication on the Internet that enables links to work

Hyper text link - text that enables you to click on it and link to another place on the Internet (usually displayed underlined on the screen)

Internet - computer networks that are connected via the massive worldwide electronic network

ISP/Internet Service Provider - a company that provides Internet access to customers. AOL is the most commonly known ISP in the U.S.

JPG/JPEG/Joint Photographic Experts Group (pronounced jay-peg) - acronym for a graphics format that is generally used for fine art displayed on the Internet

Junk mail - unwanted solicitations by e-mail

Keywords - "hidden" words used to help a search engine identify your web page

Link - a connection between two sites on the Internet

Menu bar - usually on the top or left side of a website; shows the various areas on the site you can link to; same as Scrollbar

Meta tags - keywords that a web designer encodes into a page. Search engines use these words to index the website.

Modem - a computer device that connects to a phone line and allows communicaton between computers and with the WWW

Navigation bar - same as Menu bar

Net - short for Internet

Newbie - someone new to the online world

Newsgroup - an online message board that focuses on a particular subject

Online - connected to the Internet

Page - the basic unit of which a website is made

Page header - the design at the top of an Internet page; often the company's logo

Password - a combination of letters or numbers known only by the user, which allows access to secured areas of the Internet

PDF/Portable Document Format - a computer format that saves a document in page layout and is readable by Acrobat Reader (a software program)

Peripheral - an electronic device that is used by your computer but not contained within its hardware (for example, an external modem)

Post - upload data onto a website

Proprietary server - a large ISP server such as AOL, Prodigy, Compuserve

Publish - upload data onto a website

Scroll bar - usually on the top or left side of a website; shows the various areas on the site you can link to; same as Menu bar

Search engine - a website that searches the Internet for requested information from keywords or phrases. Yahoo is an example.

Secured site - it takes a secret code to enter this site, thus protecting transfer of credit card data or other confidential information

Signature - a block of information used to sign the end of an e-mail; usually includes name, company name and other important information

SMTP/Simple Mail Transfer Protocol - guides the transmission of electronic mail through the Internet. You might notice this acronym when setting up your e-mail system.

Snail mail - United States post office mail, i.e., slow mail

Software - a program that runs some functions of your computer

Spam - unwanted and unsolicited e-mail

Spider - search engine device that crawls through websites to gather information

Splash page - the entryway into your website; often has flashes, music, and other bells and whistles taking extra time to download; often irritating to visitors!

Surfer - a person browsing the net

Thumbnail - a small version of a picture on a website that links to a larger version

Traffic - the number of visitors to your website

Upgrade - the newest version of a software program

Upload - the process of sending files onto the Internet

URL/Uniform Resource Locator - the standardized format used for an Internet address—for example, artmarketing.com is ArtNetwork's URL.

Virus - a destructive program that is usually transferred over a modem or diskette and infects parts of a computer system, causing it to crash, malfunction or lose data

Visitor - a person browsing the net

Watermark - digital watermark that imprints a copyright message on images, visible when printed, imperceptible on-screen, traceable on the Internet

Web designer - author or designer of web pages (see page 60)

Web marketing consultant - versed in marketing and advertising on the web

Web master - technical engineer of web pages (see page 59)

World Wide Web/WWW - the rules, procedures and programs allowing files to travel across the Internet and to create links of words, pictures and sounds

Zine - an electronic publication

❏ Buy a computer with a modem.

❏ Learn how to use the computer.

❏ Invest in a telephone connection that will not interfere with your regular calls.

❏ Start using the lingo of the Internet.

ACTION PLAN

_____

_____

_____

_____

_____

_____

_____

_____

RECOMMENDED READING

A Few Scanning Tips _by Wayne Fulton_

Internet 101 for Dummies _by John Levine_

Netlaw: Your Rights in the Online World _by Lane Rose_

Real World Scanning and Halftones _by David Blatner and Glenn Fleishman_

Chapter 2
You've Got E-Mail

Setting up e-mail

Sending and receiving e-mail

Doing business via e-mail

Broadcasting

The medium is the message. Marshall McCluen

SETTING UP E-MAIL

In order to use e-mail, you must first subscribe to an Internet Service Provider.

INTERNET SERVICE PROVIDER/ISP

An Internet Service Provider, sometimes called an ISP, has a big computer that allows users to store information, sort of like a post office box. ISPs abound in every city. You've probably seen large signage all over your own town advertising them. For a fee of $9 - 20 per month, an ISP will give you a local telephone number (sometimes an 800 number) to dial via your computer modem and connect to the Internet.

Your ISP will ask you to choose an e-mail address. The address will look like this:

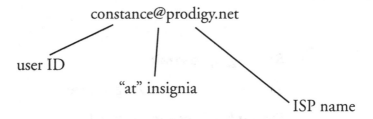

All e-mail addresses have an "@" separating the user ID and ISP name.

Your ISP also will give you the necessary computer software and instructions to connect to the Internet. You may be able to download the software from an Internet site if you already have a connection. Once you've installed that software, you're just a click away from sending an e-mail message.

CHOOSING YOUR E-MAIL ADDRESS

Choosing an appropriate e-mail address is important. Have your address be your first name, last name, first and last name, first initial and last name, company name or some description of your art style. If the name you choose matches your real name or your company name, it is much easier for people to remember. Keep your address short and simple: Don't use dots or periods, dashes or slashes, commas, underlines or numbers. No unusual spaces, capitals or characters. It should be easy to spell and remember.

➤ If you haven't used a middle initial in the past, don't start using it in your e-mail address.

➤ If you normally use a nickname, use that in your e-mail address.

GOOD ADDRESSES	BAD ADDRESSES
constance@prodigy.net	c@prodigy.net
constancesmith@prodigy.net	ConstanceSmith@prodigy.net
csmith@prodigy.net	blond@prodigy.net
artnetwork@prodigy.net	artnet@prodigy.net
artmarketing@prodigy.net	art-marketing@prodigy.net

Put your e-mail address on all of your promotional materials: letterhead, business card, ads, flyers, etc.

SENDING AND RECEIVING E-MAIL

E-mail machines:
An alternative to a computer is an e-mail machine. Don't go this route! Now that you're marketing your art and are serious about your art career, your business will need a computer.

So you've subscribed to an ISP and chosen a good e-mail address. Before you're able to send e-mail, you will need some "browser software" (not the same software you received from your ISP). Browser software is a computer program that enables you to read e-mail. Most new computers come installed with browser software such as Outlook Express and Eudora (both of which are used specifically for e-mail purposes) or Netscape Navigator, which can be used both for e-mail and surfing the Internet. If you don't have a newer computer, you will need to purchase a browser software program from your local computer store. Usually they cost no more than $19.95.

But how do you know what browser you prefer if you've never used one? Ask your friends. See what their comments are. Since Netscape works with e-mail as well as Internet access, we like that one.

Read the user manual that comes with your new browser software. It will teach you everything you need to know. With your browser software program open, the manual can be accessed on your computer. Pull down the "Help" tool at the top of your navigator bar. Under "Help" you will find an index of topics to choose from. You will be able to print or read the info on your computer screen.

Set a goal regarding installing and learning your new browser software. Give yourself enough time. A two- or three-hour time frame for installation and familiarization ought to be enough.

Your browser software manual will tell you:

➤ How to set up your e-mail

➤ How to send a friend or business associate an e-mail

➤ How to send a group of people the same e-mail with one click

➤ How to receive e-mail

➤ How to save names to an address book

➤ How to send BCCs and what they are

The e-mail you send to a friend or business sits in a virtual bin until the person downloads it onto his own computer. He can open his individual pieces of e-mail at his convenience.

➤ You can save e-mail.

➤ You can forward copies of e-mails to other people.

➤ You can copy contents of e-mail to other software programs you use.

➤ You can print out your e-mail as a hard copy.

➤ You can click on the sender's address and save it to your address book.

AUTOMATIC SIGNATURES

Set up your e-mail to automatically "sign" your name. To set up your automatic signature, consult your browser manual. An automatic signature can include your name and/or a quote, and/or a link to your website. Keep it short and memorable.

A sample automatic signature could look like this:

Visit http://artmarketing.com for all your art marketing needs

By clicking on the underlined portion, the reader will be taken to that site on the Internet

E-MAILING A SAMPLE OF YOUR ARTWORK

To send an image of your artwork via e-mail to a prospective client, you will first need to transfer the image into a 'jpg' format (detailed information about creating a jpg is in Chapter 5, page 54).

TIPS

➤ If you want an associate or friend to open a specific page on the Internet, type in "http" before the URL: i.e., http://artmarketing.com (it will appear underlined when they receive it). All they need do is click on the underlined text and that page will open up. (They must be connected to the Internet.)

Present yourself as the artist you want to be, whether you've reached your goal or not.

➤ If you're browsing the Internet and come across a page you would like someone else to see, pull down the "File" menu, then choose "Send Page," type in the recipient's e-mail address and hit "Send."

➤ You can type e-mail messages when you are off-line (not connected to the Internet). Save them by clicking the top left square on the message box. This will put the message into your draft folder. When you go back online, you can open the messages in your draft folder and send your e-mail.

➤ Most browser programs allow you to type the first few letters of a name in the "To" box, and the browser will fill in the rest of the address if you have saved it in your e-mail address book. If there are several "Michaels" in your e-mail address book, then the browser will pull up a list of Michaels to choose from. Click on the correct one and send.

To reply to an e-mail message someone has sent you, hit "Reply"; a new screen pops up with the sender's address in the outgoing slot. Just type in your reply and hit "Send." If your software is set up appropriately, it will also return the original e-mail script to the recipient, so the person will know to what you have replied!

JUNK MAIL

The downside to e-mail is the infamous junk mail that you will receive. If you are receiving a lot of junk mail, ask your server if they have a program for editing it. Often, junk mail remover software is embedded in the program you use for your e-mail. Check under "Tools," "Help," "Spam" or "Filters" for the location. Look for such software at www. shareware.com if your program or server cannot help you.

Be sure to not let the e-mail or broadcast you send out appear as if it is junk mail. Type a subject line that the sender will recognize.

DOWNLOADING

Downloading is the process of copying a document onto your computer from the Internet or an e-mail. Never download a document or attachment unless you know who has sent it, as viruses can enter your computer system in this manner.

ATTACHMENTS

You can "attach" a document or jpg (picture of your artwork) to an e-mail by clicking on the "attachment" icon in the navigator bar of your browser.

If you have the program "Stuff-It," use it to make an attachment compact so it goes faster over the web.

TIPS

➤ Check your e-mail daily.

➤ Try to respond to e-mails promptly. For some reason, people expect that! I guess they think we're all sitting at our computers all the time.

➤ You can retrieve old e-mails from the "Trash" or "Sent" file if you have not permanently deleted them. These files can be sorted by date, subject, sender, etc.

➤ Use spell check on all your e-mails.

DOING BUSINESS VIA E-MAIL

Collection of potential client names should be a primary concern. That's why you'll want to start an e-mail address book of potential clients. Any individual collector or business sending you a message is worthy of recontacting.

ADDRESS BOOKS

As people start communicating with you via e-mail, you can save their address and create a mailing list or "address book." Create various categories to store your e-mail addresses. As an artist, you would have an address book for your personal use (friends, relatives, tennis buddies, etc.), and one for your business (consultants, gallery owners, interior designers, publishers, suppliers, art stores, etc.). Your software manual will explain how to save an e-mail address into an address book.

GATHERING NAMES

➤ Research art magazines for ads from galleries, publishers and consultants. Most often, e-mail addresses are included in their ad. Type these e-mail addresses into the appropriate section of your address book.

➤ Another method of getting e-mail addresses is by purchasing a compiled list from a company. If you are using a list that you've purchased—of people who have not previously been in contact with you—you will need to use a clever approach to get them to open your e-mail. Inevitably, purchased lists are more generic than those you've taken the time to create yourself. At ArtNetwork, we've found our in-house e-mail lists (names we've gathered from visitors) to be the best.

6:1 rule
It takes six times as many dollars to bring in a new customer as it does to retain a current one.
80:20 rule
20% of your customers make up 80% of your business.

THE LOOK OF MESSAGES

Just because a message looks good when you click "send" doesn't mean the format will look the same when it is received on someone else's computer.

To minimize odd-looking e-mails:

➤ Avoid italic type.

➤ Keep lines no longer than 55-60 characters.

➤ If you are sending multiple addresses, use BCCs.

➤ Send a sample copy to your own computer and check out spelling, links, etc., before broadcasting to your in-house list.

BROADCASTING

Did you know that you can send the same message to all the people in your address book with one click? A message that you send to multiple e-mail addresses is called a "broadcast." It is one more way for your artwork to reach potential clients.

You can inform your patrons of upcoming shows, tell them about new artwork (including a picture of your work), wish them a happy holiday, etc. A broadcast should occur no more than every four weeks. Try to create messages that will intrigue your clients. Make the message your "poem." Spend some discretionary time composing your broadcast.

Do you love to critique movies or novels? Clients might like to hear an artist's view of a movie they were considering watching. Do you have information that would help an emerging collector make better purchase choices? Have you visited an art museum that your client might like to travel to? You could review it and give your impression. Be creative, inspirational, personal and mysterious. You'll have them hooked. When you finally meet this e-mail client at an opening reception you have in town, you will have a special connection.

YOUR BROADCAST SHOULD INCLUDE:

➤ A link to your site (if you have one). Make sure it links properly: Send it to yourself and check the link. Does it link to where it is supposed to?

➤ A photo of yourself or your artwork

➤ A message that is brief and easy to read

➤ A subject line that is distinct and doesn't sound like junk mail

➤ A notice to un-subscribe if desired

SAMPLE UNSUBSCRIBE NOTICES

➤ NOTICE: We are currently updating our mailing list. If you no longer wish to receive these e-mail updates, please hit reply and type REMOVE FROM LIST in subject line. If you have already requested that your name be removed from the list, please excuse our oversight as we work through updating our list. Thank you. <info@artmarketing.com>   http://artmarketing.com

➤ To unsubscribe, reply to this email with the word REMOVE in the subject line.

SUBJECT LINE

Subject line is key. If you don't choose an appropriate "subject," your e-mail might get dumped in the trash by the recipient, especially when you do a broadcast. Take notice of what words are in a subject line that gets you to open the e-mail.

GOOD SUBJECT LINES	BAD SUBJECT LINES
Artist exhibition	Win $3K
International exhibition	Info
Living artist news	Better than ever
Local gallery event	No fail

If you keep your e-mail fun, informative and lively, your recipient will be hungry for future messages.

TIPS

➤ Be sure to use BCC/blind carbon copy when sending to several people. If you don't use BCC, then all the e-mail addresses will be viewable to all the recipients!

➤ It can take six to eight e-mail contacts before someone starts to recognize your name and message. Consistency and persistence work best.

➤ Make it easy for the recipient of your communication to arrive at your website. Your automatic signature should take care of this.

➤ Keep e-mails short and direct.

➤ Don't broadcast more than once every four weeks, and make sure each one is new and interesting.

➤ As the final check for your e-mail broadcast, address it to your own e-mail address. When it downloads onto your computer, open and verify that there are no typos, the links work and content is correct. When you've verified all that, it is ready to broadcast.

If you have e-mailed to an address that doesn't exist, your e-mail will be returned to you saying "Domain Unknown." You will see that either you have typed the address incorrectly or perhaps the person has changed his address, so you will need to delete it from your address book.

❑ Sign up with an ISP.

❑ Decide on a good e-mail address.

❑ If your computer did not come with it, buy browser software and read the manual.

❑ Install a signature in your e-mail program.

❑ E-mail a friend.

❑ Notify business associates of your new e-mail address.

❑ Start compiling address books by collecting e-mail addresses of various artworld professionals from ads in magazines.

❑ Create an e-mail for a broadcast.

❑ Broadcast and keep track of the results.

❑ Add your e-mail address to your letterhead, as well as to any literature and Yellow Page ads.

❑ Publish an e-mail newsletter.

❑ Send a discount coupon to your clients via e-mail.

ACTION PLAN

_____

_____

_____

_____

_____

_____

_____

_____

_____

_____

Chapter 3
Surfing the Web

Research

People finders

Chat rooms

Great things do not just happen by impulse, but are a succession of small things linked together. Vincent Van Gogh

RESEARCH

Now that you are connected online to receive and send e-mail, you are a simple step away from surfing the web. Your browser manual will, once again, help you learn how to access the Internet. Learning how to move around the Internet is simple.

CONDUCTING A SEARCH

You can find information on just about any topic you can think of on the Internet.

The way to find a website that contains particular information is by "asking" a "search engine" to locate "XXX info."

Search engines make money through advertisers placing banners within their site as well as with pay-per-click clients.

Search engines wander through the Internet, constantly looking at new sites. They record this information so that when we go online and ask for info, their database downloads what we are searching for onto a list.

You might come to find that there is a particular search engine most accommodating to your needs—in my case, I like Alta Vista, Google and Yahoo the best. If you don't find what you are looking for through one search engine, try another.

To arrive at a search engine, either click on "Search" in the navigator bar or type in one of the search engines' names in the "Go to" line.

EXAMPLE OF SEARCH

I want information on ice-carving competitions. I can type in my search: ice carving, ice carving competitions, art of ice, art of ice carving, etc.

For my first attempt, I type (in quotes) "ice carving competitions" in the search engine. I receive 97 results from this search. I can decide from the short synopsis under each entry displayed which sites I want to browse.

When I do a second search for "ice carving competition" (non-plural), I get 5,684 results!

If you know the URL, all you need do is type it in the "location" line. You might need to add "www." before the URL.

I decide to try "art of ice" and get 17 results.

Save your search results page as a bookmark. You can then bring up this page at another time and continue to investigate the topic. Your search page will remain intact as a bookmark, and as long as you are online, you will be able to locate any of the results.

TIPS

➤ When you type in a phrase for a search, put it in quotes—for example, "art marketing." You will receive a more specific response from your inquiry than if you did not use quotes.

➤ Always do your searches in lowercase letters. When I did a search of "ART OF ICE" in all caps, I got zero results. With lower case I got 17!

➤ Be specific in your choice of words. For a more specific search, add a "+" before the most important word in your search—"+art of ice." The result will be more targeted.

➤ Did your search bring up a lot of extraneous sites? To eliminate those, put a "-" sign before the word you don't want in your search, i.e., "+art -craft of ice." This will bring up pages that **do not** contain the word "craft."

➤ If you want the word "art" to include variations such as artist, arts, artwork, put an asterisk after the word art: "art* -craft of ice."

➤ To quickly return to a web page you visited a few minutes ago: Click the "back button" on your navigator bar. You will see a list of the last few pages you have browsed through and the title of each page. Click the one to which you want to return.

WHAT YOU CAN RESEARCH

You can research all sorts of information related to your personal or business needs. For example, you can plan a vacation, look up medical information, research school courses, check out what is going on in your hometown, follow the news, and more. The list is endless.

➤ You can research other artists' sites too—there are thousands. See how they have set up their site and what you like and dislike about it. See what other artists are doing creatively.

➤ Shop for almost anything you need (or want and don't need) on the net.

When you see a company's e-mail address such as <xxxx@artmarketing.com>, it inevitably means that www.artmarketing.com is their domain address. It also means that as long as this company doesn't neglect to pay the annual fee for this address, they will be able to keep their e-mail address and URL forever, no matter where they move physically.

Spending at least one hour per week researching on the web will increase your sales. Create an e-mail list for broadcasting to consultants, licensing agents, galleries, publishers, collectors and more.

➤ Find lists of art competitions on the net at www.artdeadline.com.

➤ Research art publications, art marketing sites, web marketing sites, web design sites—the list goes on and on!

➤ You can find links to many types of art-related sites at www.artmarketing.com/links:

Art search engines	Auctions	Books, art-related
Consultants/reps	Copyright info	Framing
Galleries	Grants	Insurance
Jobs	Legal info	Libraries, art
Licensing agents newsletters	Lighting	Magazines,
Museums	Online galleries	Organizations, art
Printers	Private art studios	Publishers
Residencies	Resources	Shipping
Slide services	Software	Supplies and catalogs
Taxes	Theft and fraud	Travel

Getting disconnected suddenly from the Internet is a common and frustrating problem. If it persists over a long period of time, call and complain to your ISP.

SETTING PREFERENCES

Preferences is the feature on your computer that allows you to "direct" your software to do what you want it to do. Be sure to read about how to set up preferences in your user manual. You can find out how to set your preferences in your user manual so your Internet browser will open up to your own home page (or anywhere you choose).

PEOPLE FINDERS

Not only can you find information (and lots of it) on any topic, but you can also find people. You've probably heard of long-lost relatives being located through the Internet. If your lost relative or friend has an e-mail address, mostly likely you will be able to locate him.

I looked up someone I hadn't heard from in 25 years. There were 200 people by the same name, so I wasn't sure what to do. I picked the names without middle initials, to start with. One e-mail came back immediately, saying that it was an out-of-date e-mail address. Three months later I received an e-mail from my second inquiry. By the response they gave, I could tell it was the person I had been looking for. I was totally surprised. It could never have happened without the Internet.

Recently I received a call from a person who had paid $30 to search for an old friend. They were given my home phone number because the person had lived at my address previously. The Internet search company sent the inquirer my telephone number because it was the current phone number connected to that address. I happened to know the person who had lived in the house before me and was able to connect the inquirer to the person. Her search had started with a five-year-old address and phone number from another state.

Google, a popular search engine, has implemented a new feature that allows a user to type someone's telephone number into the search bar, hit enter, and get a name, address and map to their house! Search with forward slash and dash, i.e. 530/XXX-XXX, and hit enter. If a number is not publicly listed, the address will not appear. If you want to block Google from divulging your private information, do a search for your number, then click on the telephone icon next to your phone number. You will see a link where you are allowed to remove your number, under the title "Phone Book" at the bottom of the section.

Do a search for "people finder" and you will receive a list of companies who you can pay (from $9.95-59.95) to do a more thorough search:
- *people.yahoo*
- *altavista*
- *USSearch*

E-MAIL ACRONYMS

FCFS - first come first served

EOM - end of message

BRB - be right back

TMI - too much information

IMC - to whom it may concern

ROTFL - rolling on the floor laughing

PPD - postage paid

BTW - by the way

NRN - no reply necessary

LOL - laughing out loud

IMO - in my opinion

CHAT ROOMS

Besides being the world's largest library, the Internet is also the world's biggest entertainment lounge. You can find "rooms" in which to exchange ideas about art, marketing, or almost any other topic you desire. These rooms that hold conversations happening in "real time" are called chat rooms. Chat rooms can be a way of introducing people to your website.

➤ Lead a chat on a site that needs an artist's advice: interior designers, corporations, printers, art councils, etc. These types of peripheral contacts often lead, over time, to purchasers for your art.

➤ Maybe you can locate a group of collectors from your local museum site, or maybe you can start or sponsor a chat room with your local museum.

➤ Try www.chatway.com

FORUMS

A forum is similar to a chat room but usually doesn't happen in "real" time. You can post a message or question, and it might get answered later when someone is online and reads it.

➤ Try www.gossamer-threads.com or www.discusware.com/discus.com.

NEWSGROUPS

A newsgroup is a discussion group about a single topic. Find topics related to your artwork or interests, then contribute something to the conversations that take place. When you send your e-mail with its automatic signature, people will recognize that you are an artist.

➤ Try www.dejanews.com.

E-GROUPS

A group of participants with a similar interest carry on questions and answers over long periods of time. For instance, when my sister and I were considering going to Peru, she sent a general question to her travel e-group and got great responses from very experienced travelers.

➤ Try www.digichat.com or www.topica.com.

ACTION PLAN

_____

_____

_____

_____

_____

_____

_____

_____

_____

_____

❏ Conduct a search for galleries, corporate art consultants, interior designers, art competitions, grants, licensors and more.

❏ Reserve a hotel or make a reservation on an airline's website.

❏ Find out about art marketing classes on the Internet.

❏ View other artists' sites (and send e-mail comments).

❏ Search for an old friend or long-lost relative.

❏ Chat at an artists' forum or chat room.

RECOMMENDED READING

Clicking Through by _Jonathan Ezor_

Chapter 4
Exhibiting Online

Online exposure

URL acquisition

Don't oppose forces, use them.   Richard B Fuller

ONLINE EXPOSURE

You will find online galleries that specialize in selling a particular genre of art—portraits, landscapes, animals, equine, abstract, etc. Use your favorite search engine to locate them:
- *californiaart*
- *chinese-art*
- *ecologicalart.net*
- *marineart*
- *newyorkartists.net*

For artists not familiar with the web, the simplest way to display artwork online is to be part of an "online gallery," sometimes called cyber galleries. With an online gallery you pay an annual subscription fee. Usually, the pages within an online gallery are "pre-formatted" (all the same layout), allowing it to offer a low-cost service. Generally, an online gallery charges between $100-300 per year to show 4-10 images and a bio.

When you list with an online gallery, you have the advantage of sharing its online traffic. But remember, if the gallery has 200 artists listed, you will face competition in its index. Online galleries do not promote each artist's artwork, but invite potential clients to the gallery index, which lists all participating artists. You might need to do some PR yourself (see Chapter 6) to get started.

To see what an online gallery looks like, go to www.artmarketing.com/gallery. You will arrive at the alphabetical index. You can click on the style index and see the artists listed by medium and style.

BEFORE YOU CHOOSE AN ONLINE GALLERY

➤ View a gallery online to see what it looks like, how it functions. Browse around a bit.

➤ Do search engines find the gallery site readily? Do a search.

➤ Do search engines find an artist in the gallery readily? Do a search.

➤ Where does the online gallery advertise to bring in clients to view their artists' pages? Ask them.

➤ Who is actually coming to the site: buyers of art, collectors, the art trade, artworld professionals, other artists, the general public? Ask them.

➤ How many hits per month does it receive?

DRAWBACKS OF ONLINE GALLERIES

➤ Each time you want to update your pages, you have to send in a slide and pay a fee.

➤ With 100+ artists listed in the gallery, there is some competition. That also means, however, that those 100 artists are sending their clients to the online gallery, which could ultimately lead them to seeing your artwork.

ONLINE ART SERVERS

Online art servers are interactive websites where you can upload your artwork directly from your computer to the Internet. Online art servers are user-friendly, charge a monthly fee, and enable you to change your own pages at your whim. In a sense, you become your own web master. Usually, there is a monthly charge. One example is www.art-exchange.com.

BRICK-AND-MORTAR GALLERIES

If you are part of a brick-and-mortar (traditional) gallery, your work most likely will be shown on that gallery's website. Unless you have an exclusive contract, you might want to list your work elsewhere, as well.

NET REPS

Somewhat like a brick-and-mortar gallery, these sites require your work to be juried in before they will represent you. Sites that jury in an artist are what we have dubbed "net reps." Often, they will have the artist sign an exclusive contract for Internet sales. Acting like live reps, they advertise in consumer and trade publications to sell the artwork they have listed online. Generally, they take a percentage of sales, much like a traditional gallery. Most of these reps require that you do not show anywhere else on the Internet. Consider this option carefully if that is one of their requirements.

LEASEART.COM

Did you know that a corporation can write off up to 30% of the lease price on a piece of art by leasing-to-own? Leaseart.com's sales pitch is based on that idea. Check this site out. It might open a new venue for your art.

Net reps
art4net
allaboutart
artdial
artfaces
artincontext
artistimages
artmarketing
artonweb
artoutthere
artshow
artzoo
art-exchange
barewalls
b17
centralarray
collectfineart
easyart
fine-art
fineartsite
gallerypage
guild
justoriginals
livvnart
mindsisland
myartonline
nextmonet
nothingbutart
paintingsdirect
passion4art
portfolios
soflaartwork
solidexpressions
thegallerychannel
wwar
visualize
watercolor-online

URL ACQUISITION

Most likely, a gallery contract will not prevent you from having a website, but it might preclude you from selling on your site.

If you decide to have a web designer create a website for you, be prepared to pay between $300-1000 for the initial design. An artist recently told us he paid $3000 for 6 pages! Plan $50-100 per month for updates.

If you don't want to use one of the exhibition methods just described, but would rather create your own site, the first thing you'll need to do is apply for a URL/Uniform Resource Locator/ Internet address. Every website on the Internet has its own specific URL or address.

Even if you are using an online gallery presently to exhibit your work, it could be wise to apply for a URL. By the time you are ready to use it, your ideal URL may have been acquired by someone else.

IDEAL URLS

➤ Go to www.idomains.com or www.register.com and enter your chosen URL to see if it is already taken. If your first choice is taken, you will be shown variations on the name you chose.

➤ Think carefully about the name you ultimately choose. When ArtNetwork wanted to acquire artnetwork.com, it was already taken. We could have purchased artnetwork1.com, artwork.com, networkart.com, theartnetwork.com. After several days of considering a variety of URLs, artmarketing.com seemed to be the most appropriate. We are still happy with this choice. In fact, we have considered changing our company name to Artmarketing.com!

➤ When choosing a URL, follow the same tips as when selecting an e-mail address (Chapter 2, pages 22-23).

➤ Whatever letters or numbers you choose, your URL can be no longer than 67 characters—but 67 characters is much too long.

Try to make your URL as short as possible, but more importantly, make it:

➤ easy to remember

➤ easy to pronounce (which you'll do a lot of on the phone), and

➤ easy to spell.

An extra dash or unusual character will make it more difficult to verbalize, as well as more difficult to type correctly.

➤ You can apply for and receive a URL without having to publish a web page for years. As long as you pay your annual subscription fee, you can retain that URL domain name.

EXPIRED DOMAIN LISTINGS

If the name you would like to use for your URL is already taken, you will need to brainstorm a different one. Take a look at these sites, where you will find lists of expired URLs that have once again become available (i.e., the owner did not renew their usage).

domainmart   iwantmy   nameprotect

redhotdomainnames   unclaimeddomains

WHERE TO SIGN UP

There are several places you can register for a URL, with a variety of fees ranging from $35-75 per year. Don't let a company register your URL for you, because ultimately they will own it!

networksolutions   internic

netnamesusa   onehost

ISP HOSTS

Once your site is designed, you will need to upload and park it on the Internet.

Similar to an ISP for e-mail, you will need an ISP to host your website. (You won't need an ISP if you participate in an online gallery, however.) Sometimes the same ISP host can connect your e-mail and your website. Call your e-mail ISP to see what they offer. Costs vary according to how many pages you post. ArtNetwork's ISP server charges $50 per month (for about 1000 pages). As a small user, perhaps with 20-40 pages, you might pay $10 per month. AOL users, for instance, can get 10mg of storage (several hundred pages) for free.

ArtNetwork's ISP host, www.festivalnet.com, provides space for small companies. Festivalnet.com has friendly service and advice. The owner, Kurt Irmiter, runs an arts and crafts-related website as well. He can help you design and install pages, send press releases, install cgi code for shopping carts or order forms, promote your

Auto responder is an e-mail that automatically replies to an incoming e-mail, stating that you are out of the office for a period of time and cannot respond immediately.

site to search engines, or set up a secured site. As an artist, this is the kind of service that you need.

ISP HOSTS SHOULD OFFER:

➤ Auto responders

➤ Secured server option for payment transactions

➤ Design assistance at an hourly rate

➤ Customized forms such as feedback, guest books or order forms

➤ Low modem-to-user ratio. If this is too high, your site traffic will move slowly

➤ FTP access

➤ CGI bin or shopping cart software

➤ E-mail boxes for your various aliases, such as info@artmarketing.com, support@artmarketing.com, etc.

➤ Statistical reports

ISP HOSTS

afternic	A-1hosting	buydomains
domainit	easyspace	festivalnet
globalspacesolutions	hostsave	interland
register	registernames	simpleurl
verisign	whois	

FREE HOSTING

The old adage, "You get what you pay for," has never been more true than when it comes to free ISP hosting. There are free ISP hosts; however, there are many drawbacks. We recommend that if you are going to go to the trouble of having a URL, pay for the storage of it. Don't use a free hosting service.

DRAWBACKS OF FREE ISP HOSTS

➤ Many require putting their advertising banners on your site—a major pain to your customers.

➤ Customer service is poor, if not outright nil!

➤ Free hosts tend to go out of business overnight.

➤ They've been known to become commercial. You end up paying for the space.

➤ The URL they give you is generally so long that you would not be able to say it over the phone easily.

Free web-hosting services:
- *angelfire*
- *bizland*
- *doteasy*
- *dreamwater*
- *freeservers*
- *geocities*
- *hypermart*
- *netcolony*

The ultimate purpose of your art site is exposure.

ACTION PLAN

_____

_____

_____

_____

_____

_____

_____

_____

_____

_____

_____

❑ Check out some of the online galleries.

❑ Check out some Internet reps.

❑ Check out leaseart.com.

❑ Acquire a URL, if not for immediate use, then for future possibilities.

Chapter 5
Selling Art On eBay

by Susan F Greaves

Never pass up an opportunity, nor put it off until tomorrow.

INTRODUCTION

As an artist living in a small city, most of my efforts to market my work have had limited success. Countless hours were spent hauling and hanging work, sending portfolios to galleries, entering slides in shows, and framing and shipping work at massive expense.

In March 1999, I began putting my work on online auctions, hardly believing that anyone would buy art from a computer screen. By the end of seven months, I had sold over 125 paintings at an average of $240 per piece to collectors and dealers from California to Florida and even in Germany and Portugal! That was an additional $30,000 in sales that year that I would not have had otherwise. Soon, I began telling artist friends of my good fortune and showing them how to place their work.

SELLING ON EBAY IS DIFFERENT

There is nothing to compare with the audience that 30 million registered users of eBay open to artists! Many of those perusing the fine art listings are art dealers. Why else would they buy so many pieces that they could paper their walls with those paintings alone? In addition, many people who eagerly search through the eBay listings have never set foot in a fine art gallery. I suppose that eBay is less threatening, but the eventual benefit to artists is that selling to those individuals builds the future of the fine art market.

HOW THE PROCESS WORKS

➤ First, you prepare images of your artwork. You will learn in detail how to do that—all the choices available and various costs of each.

➤ Next, you fill out records for each artwork—a form is provided on the next page—that will let you record each item's progress.

➤ Then, you will submit the artwork to eBay.

➤ Lastly, you will be guided through post-auction activities, whether for a sale where you collect payment from the buyer and ship the work, or for strategies to put the item up for auction again.

Copyright Susan F Greaves

WORKSHEET

Title _____

Size _____   Medium _____

Retail $ _____   Shipping _____

Prices _____   Weeks   1-3 _____

| | | | 4-5 _____ |
| | | | |

Image of artwork

4-5 _____

6-7 _____

8-9 _____

Start	End	Auction #
1		
2		
3		
4		
5		
6		
7		
8		
9		

SOLD TO

Buyer name _____

Buyer feedback

User ID _____

E-mail _____

Phone _____

Address _____

_____

Date sold _____

Bid _____

Frame? _____

Tax? _____

Shp chg _____

Total _____

Date Paid _____

Method _____

Amt Paid _____

Balance _____

Dates:

1st notification _____

Address rec'd _____

Total sent _____

Payment rec'd _____

Payment cckn _____

Date shipped _____

Ship notified _____

Inventory _____

Mailing List _____

Posted _____

Feedback given _____

You will be aiming for volume, not high prices on a few pieces.

The psychology of selling artwork in Internet auctions is very different from the established gallery system.

PROS AND CONS

➤ Expect to save lots of time and money by not framing, not mailing invitations, not paying for receptions, not hanging, not packing (we recommend that you use a shipper), and not paying for shipping to and fro.

➤ Expect to see your work grow because you will have time and, expecially, motivation to work.

➤ In exchange for bypassing the middle man, the buyer expects near-wholesale prices. Most of your sales will be to art dealers, so your work ultimately will enter the market at retail. Be humble. You'll gain!

➤ Do not expect to sell every artwork the first week it is placed on auction. It may take several weeks for the right work, the right buyer, and the right price to come together.

➤ When you start, do not expect bidding to go a lot higher than the starting bid. In time, bidders will look for your work and more bids will be placed.

Stay focused! You will be tempted to try every Internet offer that comes along. Other than keeping yourself informed about eBay changes and upcoming eBay events, use your time to produce artwork, not to chase rainbows!

Follow these next six steps and you will be auctioning your work on eBay in a jiffy.

STEP I - ORGANIZE YOUR COMPUTER

Set up folders for your eBay activities.

➤ Create a New Folder on your hard drive and name it eBay.

➤ Open the folder.

➤ Click on the New Folder icon at the top of that window, creating another new folder within the first.

➤ Name it Images to Prep.

➤ Create more new folders within the eBay folder, naming them:

Prepped images

Statements

Collectors

Form letters

Forms

STEP II - CREATE A RECORD FOR EACH ARTWORK

Photocopy the form on page 53 and fill out one for each artwork. These will go into a notebook described in Step VI.

Note: Place thumbnail image of work in rectangle area of form near top left.

STEP III - PREPARE IMAGES OF YOUR ARTWORK

Prepare images of artwork.

➤ Photograph your images.

➤ Transfer your images to your Images to Prep folder on your computer.

➤ Prepare your images and save them in your Prepped Images folder.

THE SIX STEPS

Take your photos, slides or digital images in sunlight or under color-balanced light. This will save you many reproduction headaches.If you are selling a piece framed or you are selling three-dimensional pieces, shoot them against a plain background or drape.

Always use the highest resolution your camera allows

PREPARING IMAGES

Digital Cameras - Images from a digital camera are the easiest way to get your art to a computer and then to eBay for auction.

shopping.com   mysimon.com   ebay.com

Scanned artwork - If your artwork is two-dimensional and small, you can scan it with a flatbed scanner ($50-75). Use the highest resolution possible. Place the scans in the Images to Prep folder.

Photographs - Use a flatbed scanner to scan photos onto your computer. Save the scans in your Images to Prep folder. Alternatively, you can take the photos to Kinko's or a service bureau for scanning. If you take new photos of your work, most film processing services these days will put the images on a floppy disk or e-mail them to you.

Slides - Use a flatbed scanner with a slide adapter, or a slide scanner. Alternatively, take the slides to Kinko's or a service bureau.

If you already have an extensive collection of slides of your work, an excellent alternative may be the Hewlett-Packard PhotoSmart S20 slide scanner. Next to a high-resolution digital camera, this gives the best images. To learn about it go to:

shopping.com   hpshopping.com

ebay.com   buy.com

➤ Save your images in your Images to Prep folder.

Decide what imaging program to use. Your computer or digital camera may have come with one already installed. If it is easy to use, do so. The adjustments you have to make to your images should be simple (assuming that you have taken them in good light), so a basic photo software program will suffice.

➤ Use the program that came with your digital camera.

➤ MGI PhotoSuite - The simplest version will do and it is inexpensive. Check this site: www.roxio.com/en/products/index.jhtml if you want to purchase it ($29.95)

➤ Paintshop Pro - A simplified, less expensive version is available for users such as yourself at $99 or less. Check this site: www.paintshoppro.com.

PREP

➤ Save the image. Name it. Use the title of the work in all small letters or digits without any punctuation marks or symbols, i.e., eveningintheforest.jpg

➤ Crop the image, eliminating the background if it is a two-dimensional piece.

➤ Resize the image. This will allow the image to fit the screen and load quickly.

> Maximum height: 375 pixels
>
> Maximum width: 450 pixels

➤ Adjust the image. Be sure the contrast is good and the colors are bright enough.

➤ Be sure the file extension is .jpg or .gif.

➤ Save it in your Prepped Images folder.

Copyright Susan F Greaves

STEP IV - PREPARE AUCTION DESCRIPTIONS

➤ Prepare a biography using your favorite word-processing program. This biography should be no more than six or eight sentences and should summarize your training, style, media and awards. Make it a single paragraph in block form. Name it Bio and save it in the Statements folder as "Bio."

➤ Prepare a short statement for each artwork. It should focus on why you created this artwork, where you created it, how it relates to the rest of your work, and/or any personal experience. Give the buyer something to relate to. Also include the artwork title, size, medium, whether framed or unframed and the retail price. Save each description in the Statements folder.

➤ Prepare your Master auction description. Into this you will paste specific details of each work.

This Master auction description must be in HTML, but don't let that scare you. Here's a short and simple definition of HTML.

This statement is key to the effectiveness of your ad.

HTML

HTML is the coding language used to create web pages for use on the Internet. It consists of a command enclosed in brackets, i.e., <XXX>. Some commands, like paragraph <p> and next line <br>, are needed only once. Others, like bold <b>, are needed twice to explain where to begin and where to end its application. The end symbol is a forward slash </>. The most useful HTML codes are:

<p>	paragraph
 	next line or return
<center>	begin centering text or image
</center>	stop centering text
<b>	begin bold text
</b>	end bold text

Following is a copy of the script you need to copy and paste into the Notepad program in your computer. If you are on a Mac system, you might use Simple Text or Text Editor. To copy it from an online source, go to www.pitchfordart.com/HTML_basic_ desc.htm. (Go to Start/ Programs/ Accessories/ Notepad).

TIP

It is necessary to use Notepad for text to transfer directly into the eBay form and to have it work correctly; some word-processing programs cause problems with HTML. Type your information into the parts indicated by capital letters.

<center><b>Offered by YOUR NAME
YOUR TAG LINE<p></center>YOUR STATEMENT ABOUT THIS ARTWORK<p></b>YOUR BIOGRAPHY<p>Personal checks accepted unless a buyer has unfavorable eBay feedback. COD's and money orders also accepted. The buyer will be responsible for the cost of packaging, shipping, and insurance. YOUR STATE buyers add YOUR TAX RATE% tax. </font> <b>Returns of undamaged work accepted unconditionally within 90 days of receipt. </b>Note that damage during shipping is covered by the shipping insurance. Buyer pays all shipping costs, including return shipping. International sales accepted if payment is by international money order in US dollars. International buyer is responsible for all taxes, duties, and border fees.<p><center><b>You are now invited to place your bid!</b>

➤ Save this document in your Descriptions folder. Title it Master.

➤ After typing or copying the preceding HTML, enter your name in YOUR NAME and create a tag line (like "California Plein Air Paintings") in YOUR TAG LINE. Copy and paste the biography in YOUR BIOGRAPHY and the name of your state and the tax rate.

➤ Save these changes. Then, we suggest that you lock this document. To do that, open the folder and highlight the name of the document. Right click and select Properties. Beside Attributes, put a check mark by Read Only by clicking on the box next to it.

STEP V - SUBMIT ARTWORK AND START AUCTION

➤ Register as an eBay user. Go to www.ebay.com. Click on "Register Now." Follow the instructions. You will receive an e-mail and User ID. We suggest that you change your User ID to an easy-to-remember name, like "smithart."

➤ Provide a valid credit card to eBay for the auction listing charges and commissions. Select eBay site map at the top of any eBay page. Under Seller Accounts, choose "Place or update my credit card."

➤ Go to eBay's Sell Your Item page (click on Sell at the top of any eBay page). Follow instructions, referring to the notes below.

TIPS

➤ Tell eBay that you will use their Basic Picture Services. (You will only need to pick your photo hosting service the first time you list). Under First, choose a main category, click on Art and select appropriate subcategories. Choosing a second category is optional.

➤ Enter a Title up to 55 characters for the auction, i.e., Bold Plein Air Landscape Oil Jones

➤ Add the auction description that you prepared earlier, using the Master plus the artwork statement.

➤ Leave Quantity as 1. We do not recommend Dutch auctions.

➤ Enter the highest amount you set according to the pricing strategy described in Enhancing Sales, Pricing (page 63) as the Minimum Bid.

Photo hosting service: a place on the web where you can upload and store your images.

➤ Leave the Auction Duration as seven days.

➤ Leave Reserve Price empty. We do not recommend reserves.

➤ Leave Private Auction unchanged.

➤ Select image.

➤ Select Add a Counter.

➤ Select Buyer Pays Actual Shipping Cost.

➤ Select Remember My Selling Preferences.

Proofread everything carefully. Once everything is perfect, hit Submit. Your auction has started! You will get a confirmation e-mail from eBay. When you do, copy the item number into the space provided on the worksheet. Also enter the ending date.

STEP VI   POST AUCTION

Get organized by getting a three-ring binder and dividers. Label dividers:

Sold - artwork that has been sold and is in the follow-up process

Listed - current auctions

Not Sold - artwork that has been up for auction that will be relisted

New - artwork ready to list

To Prep - artwork for which images and auction are being prepared

Hold - artwork set aside to list as part of a promotion or for other reasons

The worksheets will normally move from back to front. Any worksheet that is moved should be placed at the back of its section. Place your worksheets for the auctions you have started in Listed.

WHEN YOUR ARTWORK SELLS

These steps are represented by entries in the right column of the worksheet (page 53). The top section deals with the money involved. The second section allows you to record the dates of other actions.

➤ **Get the User ID and e-mail address of buyer.** The buyer's e-mail address will arrive in an e-mail from eBay with other information about the sale. Fill in the buyer's User ID and e-mail address on the artwork worksheet under Sold To.

➤ **Check feedback on eBay.** Go to your item listing and click on the number after the bidder's name to check his feedback. If it has negatives and is questionable, you will want to be more cautious, but this does not mean you should not sell to him. If he agrees to pay using PayPal, a certified check, or a money order, you can ship the work on receipt of payment. If he wants to send a check, you may wait for the check to clear the bank before shipping

➤ **Record the information** about the sale in the top right column of the worksheet.

➤ **Contact the buyer.** Send the e-mail form letter (page 75) to the top bidder. Formulate this letter in your word processor and save it in the Form Letters folder. Copy and paste it into your e-mail and then change the variables to fit the sale.

➤ **When you get an address,** have the artwork packed and weighed and get the total amount for packing, shipping, tracking and insurance. Notify the buyer of this amount.

➤ **Record dates** of auctions, such as first notification of buyer and total sent, on right side of worksheet. Spaces are provided for other record-keeping activities such as entering the sale in your long-term inventory, asking the buyer if he'd like to be on your mailing list, and entering the transaction in your accounting record.

POST AUCTION

IF YOUR ARTWORK DOES NOT SELL

When you are ready to relist the artwork, click on the relist button in the End of Auction e-mail you received from eBay.

➤ Make any changes in title or price as recommended by the schedule described later in Enhancing Sales.

➤ Proofread your listing carefully.

➤ When all is perfect, hit Submit. Your auction has started.

➤ When you get the e-mail confirming the listing, enter the auction item number on the worksheet as before.

PRICING

Buyers who are collectors look on eBay to avoid high gallery prices. If they are dealers, they need to get the work at wholesale or below to be able to sell it at a profit after framing and other costs. Be sure to put the gallery retail price in your descriptions. It may take several weeks to get the right price, the right artwork, and the right buyer together.

ENHANCING SALES

The single most important element for success with eBay sales is pricing correctly.

The $30,000 in sales I made were from the sale of original works from my 25-year accumulation of paintings. The sizes ranged from 8x10" to 36x48". I priced according to size starting with $85 for 8x10" and $800 for 36x48". The eBay buyers were certainly comparing size and price, and still do.

SET FOUR PRICE LEVELS FOR EACH ARTWORK

We recommend that you set your lowest minimum bid for unframed work at one-third of retail. Increase this in increments over the four levels. List the piece three times at the highest level, twice at the second level, twice at the third, and then at the lowest. More often than not, you will have sold it before it gets to the lowest. (Refer to the information about "Titles" for each price level on page 66.)

IMAGE QUALITY

➤ In focus

➤ Represents color correctly

➤ Loads quickly

DESCRIPTION

The statements about your artwork that you prepared earlier should personalize it and give the buyer something to identify with. Linking the buyer to the artist and/or artwork is most successful.

Here is an example of a simple description I used early on.

I painted this in the shade of trees covering Rio Ruidoso in New Mexico on one of the Alla Prima International's painting trips. The darks gave a sense of mystery, while the evening sun lit the bridge and the spring leaves. *Bridges to Mystery* is a 9x12″ oil, archivally adhered to a panel, and is unframed. The gallery retail for my work this size is $350.

It has been my pleasure to sell over 250 of my paintings on eBay under User IDs greavesart, pitchfordart, and sfgfineart. (Please read my feedback.) I have been painting for over 25 years, and my work has been recognized across the United States with more than 50 awards. I have been elected to signature membership in Knickerbocker Artists and Alla Prima International and juried associate membership in Oil Painters of America. Remember, all sales guaranteed. Returns cheerfully accepted!

When you price your work for sale on eBay, allow for the costs you will be saving—framing, shipping, commissions. If you do, you will have more frequent sales and larger total sales.

Copyright Susan F Greaves

Be sure your auction description answers all the questions the buyer may have:

➤ Tell why you created the piece.

➤ Give the location, season, or a story about what's depicted, an experimental method, mood, etc.

➤ What inspired the work

➤ Size

➤ Medium

➤ Retail price

➤ Print/original, edition size

➤ Shipping costs

➤ A statement about the artwork as discussed previously

➤ A short biography

➤ Link to your eBay About Me page on which you are allowed to put a link to other web pages that show your work (optional, but advised)

➤ A link to your eBay Seller List that leads buyers to your other listings on eBay (optional, but advised)

➤ Transaction details: payment methods accepted, return policy, shipping information, and international sales information

➤ How to contact you

Even though links to your seller list and contact information are at the top of the auction's page, many eBayers do not know how to use them or do not return after they have scrolled down the page. It never hurts to repeat!

START AND ENDING TIMES

Bidders find auctions on eBay in different ways. If they want to see what is newly listed, they will look at the category list that has the most recently listed items first. If they are impatient and don't want to wait a week or more to win an auction, they will choose to look at items ending in the next three hours or the next 24 hours.

Most private collectors go on eBay in the evenings and on the weekends. Dealers generally search and bid on weekdays during business hours in their time zone. It is best to list enough auctions (14 to 21) to spread them through the seller list by listing daily, morning and evening—one morning and one or two evening auctions.

➤ List one artwork priced under $100 daily in the mornings (7-day auction).

➤ List two artworks under $200 daily in the evenings (7-day auction).

➤ For works $200 or over, list them in the evenings on Wednesday and Thursday as 10-day auctions. This gives the auctions an opportunity to be seen by both weekday browsers and weekend bidders.

You should start and end most of your auctions in prime time (9-5), spreading your listings through the auction lists.

EBay also offers a picture tutorial. Click on Help at the top of any eBay page and enter "picture tutorial" in the Search Help box.

TITLES

EBay allows only 55 characters in each auction title. If you have room after entering the most important words bidders use when searching, we recommend that you use a descriptive adjective to catch the attention of those scrolling through the list.

EBay bidders also use searches to locate the artwork they want. The words you include in your title will determine in how many searches your listing will be shown. Include as many of the following (if applicable) as possible in your title:

➤ Medium

➤ On canvas or on paper

➤ General size - miniature, small, large, huge

➤ Predominant color

➤ Subject

➤ Original/print

➤ Artist's name

Determine the easiest way for your current collectors and eBay bidders to find your work. Test-search by entering your last name in any eBay search box. How many items turn up? If there are many, try your initial, a space, plus your last name or some other variation of your name or Seller ID. Place the version that shows the fewest listings in your auction titles, in your publicity materials and on your business card.

By capitalizing some of the words in the title, you make it more eyecatching.

HERE ARE FOUR TITLES FROM MY CURRENT AUCTIONS

- Greaves 24x30 STILL LIFE Floral ROSES Oil paintings
- Greaves IMPRESSIONIST ART Plein Air Oil Painting TAOS
- TAOS EXHIBITION Plein Air Oil Painting Listed Greaves
- Greaves OIL FIGURE Painting Girl Woman Original

DESCRIPTIVE WORDS

BEAUTIFUL
attractive
grand
magnificent
exquisite
good-looking
handsome
radiant
superb
fabulous
wonderful
fantastic
marvelous
aesthetic
poetic
creative
musical
exceptional
extraordinary
remarkable
excellent
splendid
engaging
luminous
sparkling
glittering
dazzling
gleaming
appealing
charming
elegant
fascinating
graceful
refined
gorgeous
comely
wonderful
superior
premium
superb
refined

BRIGHT
blazing color
burnished
flaming color
intense
infused
Colorful
bright
brilliant
resplendent
picturesque
distinctive
glamorous
vibrant
outstanding
graphic
jazzy
lively
rich
stimulating
unusual

FINE
refined
choice
quality
great
elegant
well done
uncommon
singular
exceptional
extraordinary
remarkable
excellent
superior
premium
superb
accomplished
exquisite
first-class
select
distinct

BRILLIANT
radiant
resplendent

LUMINOUS
lucent
shining
beaming
illuminated
lighted
radiant
aglow

NICE
pleasant
agreeable
pleasing
likeable
delightful
admirable

QUIET
tranquil
moody
inspirational
enticing
alluring
fetching
bewitching
seductive
desirable
fascinating

PICTURESQUE
pleasant
quaint
scenic
impressive
outstanding
imposing
striking

STRONG
important
meritorious
worthwhile
significant
powerful
convincing
imposing
energetic
mercurial
lively
vivacious
elegant

VIVID
shining
glowing
intense
realistic color

SPONTANEOUS
free
impromptu
unconstrained
energetic
vigorous
unfettered

VIBRANT
resonant
aglow
active
dynamic
upbeat
forceful
charismatic
vigorous
astir
animated
electrifying
sparkling
spirited
vivacious
arresting

LENGTH OF AUCTIONS

EBay offers 3-day, 5-day, 7-day, and 10-day auctions. Usually, 3- and 5-day auctions do not give your artwork enough exposure to be successful.

➤ Use 7-day auctions for work priced $200 and under.

➤ Use 10-day auctions ending on Saturday or Sunday for work priced over $200.

KEEP AN E-MAIL LIST

Start and continually update an e-mail list of your bidders and buyers. Divide them by interest, subject or medium. Save in your eBay Collectors folder. E-mail them from time to time to thank them for their interest, inform them of promotional weeks, convey holiday greetings, and inform them of other art shows and competitions in which you participate.

Caution: EBay can be very strict about these e-mails. Be sure you ask a bidder's permission to add him to your e-mail list. Do not overuse this list or they may consider it spamming. Be sure to include a statement such as, "If you prefer not to be on our e-mail list, hit 'reply' and type 'remove.'" This will protect you in the event of such accusations. Giving it a friendly tone will avoid most trouble.

PAYMENT METHODS

Buyers usually want to take care of payment quickly. They either want to use a credit card, pay electronically, or get the check in the mail quickly.

Most eBay buyers want to use electronic payment methods. PayPal.com is the most popular one and is very easy to use. With PayPal, the transaction can be completed in a matter of minutes so you can ship the artwork expeditiously. There is a small service charge to the seller.

PAYPAL.COM

PayPal is a wonderful Internet service and is now integrated with eBay. It collects from buyers using credit cards or bank accounts, or transfers money from their PayPal account and pays you. You, as the seller, will not need a separate merchant credit card account. You have a choice of receiving a check by mail or doing electronic transfers into your bank account. PalPal now charges a small fee for merchants, but it is well worth it.

In our experience, buyers love it because they feel more secure than they would by sending a check to an unknown person. Also, they can get their merchandise sooner.

TO SIGN UP FOR PAYPAL

Go to www.paypal.com.

Click the Sign Up button at the top.

On the next screen, fill in the fields for the Merchant Account.

Hit Submit.

If payment is by PayPal, you can let the buyer handle it (he just has to know your e-mail address) or you can go to PayPal and submit a request for payment. Hit Request Payment. PayPal will notify you by e-mail when payment is received.

BIDPAY.COM

If a buyer does not want to use PayPal.com but wants his artwork as soon as possible, he can send you a money order purchased through BidPay.com, a site operated by Western Union. You will get the money as a check in the mail, but once you get an e-mail from BidPay confirming the purchase of the money order, you can safely ship the artwork.

SCHEDULING AUCTIONS

Place a two-week interval between each of the following listing levels: 2-3, 4-5, 6-7 and 8-9.

Copyright Susan F Greaves

WEEKS 1-3

The first three times you list, you will use the highest price. For this eBay title, we have the most spaces available of the 55 maximum characters that eBay allows. Use as many searchable words as possible and a descriptive adjective like "Fine," "Glowing," "Major," etc. Check our list of descriptive words on page 67. If the work doesn't sell the first week, relist it immediately by going to its item page and clicking on "relist." (If it sells that second week, eBay will credit you for the listing fee.) If it doesn't sell after the second week, wait two weeks before listing again.

WEEKS 4-5

Begin titles with the words "New Price," alerting bidders that you've lowered the price without saying it. The majority of our sales have taken place within the first three weeks. If you consistently have to list more often, reevaluate your prices and titles. There will be some works that take the total number of weeks, but not many.

WEEKS 6-7

Begin the listing titles with "Bargain," "A Deal," or something similar, and use the lowered price at the third level.

WEEKS 8-9

Start the titles with "A Steal" or some hyperbole that says the price is the lowest.

If a piece has not sold after being listed 9 times, do not list it for 3-4 months. Often, when you start the series again, it will sell at one of the higher prices.

DAYS NOT TO LIST

Be aware of upcoming holidays and events. Do not start your listings to end on major holidays:

➤ Easter

➤ Christmas

➤ Mother's Day

➤ Thanksgiving

Surprisingly, Super Bowl Sunday is a good day for sales. Do not list heavily the two weeks before Christmas, or two weeks before quarterly taxes are due (April 15, July 15, October 15, and January 15). Other events, such as the Olympics or a national election, will cut into sales.

PLAN PROMOTIONAL WEEKS

Several times a year, list a special grouping of your work and e-mail the people on your list about it. Ideas are "New Works," "Best Paintings Week," "Equine Week," "Portrait Week." Also, include those words in your eBay titles to attract the attention of other browsers.

ADVERTISE

Even small classified ads in collectors' magazines are remarkably effective. Coordinate these with your promotional weeks. Also consider magazines related to the subject of your art. If you do waterfowl, place ads in hunting magazines, environmental magazines, etc. If you do aviation art, place ads in flying magazines, military aircraft magazines, antique and experimental aircraft magazines, etc. Send postcards to your current mailing list announcing that your work is available on eBay. Tell them the best way to search for your work (which you've found by experimenting with eBay searches). Cite this on your business card and give your Seller ID.

ADVANCED STRATEGIES

UNDER-PROMISE, OVER-DELIVER, AND REVERSE THE RISK

These are important concepts for selling on auctions. Bidders, especially those who are new to eBay, feel they are taking a risk. They do not know you and have heard horror stories about the Internet. Do not make claims that you cannot deliver!

Add something to each shipped order that the buyer did not expect. A few note cards, a small print, even reprints of articles or leftover invitations to shows that have images of your work are well received.

To reverse risk, offer a liberal return policy. The longer the return period, the better. It has been shown that the longer the return period, the larger the increase in sales.

Our Guarantee: Returns of undamaged artwork accepted within 90 days of receipt. Note that damage during shipping is covered by the shipping insurance. Buyer pays return shipping.

SHIPPING CHARGES

Shipping costs have become more and more of a concern. If at all possible, state the amount of the shipping charges in the ad. Some eBay sellers inflate the shipping fees to increase their profits. Consequently, bidders want a fixed amount they can count on before bidding, or assurance that they pay the actual cost of shipping and not an inflated "handling" fee.

The best way to ship your work is to use a professional shipper. Not only are you freed of the headaches of packing, but carriers are less likely to question claims for damage. Be sure the shipping agent is reasonable about the amount of packing necessary. Some interpret the UPS requirements for shipping art as meaning there must be two inches of bubble wrap and two layers of cardboard around an unframed quarter-sheet watercolor. In that case, it would be better to pack it yourself in foam core and send it by U.S. Priority Mail or roll it and send it in a mailing tube.

The main difference between UPS and U.S. Priority Mail is insurance claims. UPS will let you file a claim as soon as you realize something has not arrived on schedule and their tracking says it has been delivered. Priority Mail requires that you wait for 30 days to file a claim (in hopes the item will show up). This delays the conclusion of the transaction considerably. We have found that, in most cases, the cost savings was worth the unlikely complication, and we use Priority Mail whenever possible.

Here are some sources of shipping information:

www.USPS.com   www.UPS.com   www.FedEx.com

www.stamps.com

NETWORK WITH OTHER EBAY ARTISTS AND SELLERS

There's strength in numbers! Have you ever noticed that communities that have a gallery district where there are multiple galleries are more vital than those whose galleries are scattered? Take this lesson online by trading experiences, ideas, and technical tips with other artists who are selling on eBay. Sign up at eBayArtistsNetwork on www.groups.yahoo.com. Be sure to read through the archived messages.

TIME-SAVERS

Our biggest time-saver has been using one of these two preparation methods:

OPTION I

Prepare and schedule all nine weeks of auctions for each artwork at once. If an artwork sells, delete the remaining scheduled auctions.

OPTION 2

Prepare a series of four auctions per artwork (one at each price level) at the same time. Schedule them to run with a gap of seven to 10 days between the end of one and the start of the next. This moves the work through the price levels more quickly. Again, if an artwork sells, delete the remaining scheduled auctions.

AUCTION SERVICES

There are now many online auction-management services. They range in cost, speed, and complexity.

For best value, use eBay's auction listing software—TurboLister—and eBay's My eBay page to follow your auctions' progress. These are free, though there is a $.10 charge to schedule each listing to start at a future time.

EBay's Selling Manager is an inexpensive management service ($4.95 per month) and offers most of the services that other, more expensive management services offer.

OTHER AUCTION SERVICES

ManageAuctions.com   www.andale.com

Auction Hawk.com

If you do not use TurboLister or one of the other services, another way to save time is to use an ad preparation software. These allow you to use their pre-designed ads or design your own. (Be careful not to adopt a design whose flash takes attention away from your artwork.) Many auction management services include templates, or you can get a separate program such as Virtual Auction Ad Pro from www.auctionriches.com.

FORM LETTERS

Whether you use a management program or create and send your e-mails on your own, you will find that you are saying the same thing over and over. Copy, customize, and save in your Form Letters folder the following letters:

FIRST LETTER TO BUYER

Forward the eBay notification of the End of Auction and copy this letter into the accompanying e-mail.

Dear XXXXXXX,

Congratulations and thank you for your winning bid on this auction. Please send your address, preferred method of shipping, and method of payment so I can send your total and ship the work as soon as possible. Shipping charges will include packing, insurance, tracking, and shipping.

I prefer PayPal, and its use will expedite shipping. Certified checks and money orders will also expedite shipping, but shipping is delayed until I receive one of these. I will accept a personal check, but shipping is delayed further until the check clears.

I look forward to hearing from you.

Sincerely,

XXXXXXXX

SECOND LETTER TO BUYER, IF NO RESPONSE

Go to "Old Mail" and forward the eBay End of Auction notice again. Copy this letter into the accompanying e-mail.

Dear XXXXXX,

I am looking forward to completing the auction sale of my artwork, which is the eBay item in the forwarded message. Thank you again for your winning bid.

EBay policy states that the buyer and seller should make contact within three business days. This is my second notice to you. Again, I request your address, preferred method of shipping, and intended method of payment so I can send your total.

To restate, I prefer PayPal, and its use will expedite shipping. Certified checks and money orders will also expedite shipping. Shipping will be delayed until I receive one of these. I will accept a personal check, but shipping is delayed further until the check clears.

Please respond quickly. I would hate for you to miss this artwork.

Sincerely,

XXXXXXXX

LETTER RE SHIPPING METHOD AND CHARGES

If you do not put a fixed shipping amount in your auction, use the following letter to notify the buyer of the exact shipping amount.

Dear XXXXXX,

Your artwork has been packed and weighed. The fee for packing, shipping, insurance, and tracking is $_____, making your total $_____. It will be sent via _____.

Please send payment through PayPal to my e-mail address or mail it to me at (address).
The work will be sent as soon as payment is complete. I will let you know the date of shipping.

Sincerely,

XXXXX

LETTER INFORMING BUYER OF RECEIPT OF PAYMENT

Dear XXXXXX,

I received your payment today via _____(check, PayPal, etc.) for $_____ for eBay auction number _____ for my artwork titled _____. I will ship it ASAP and will let you know when it goes out.

Sincerely,

XXXXXX

LETTER INFORMING BUYER OF SHIPMENT

Dear XXXXXX,

Your artwork was shipped on _____ via _____. Please inform me of its arrival and whether it met your expectations.

Sincerely,

XXXXXX

RESOURCES

Additional help from author
www.pitchfordart.com

Announcement page:
www2.ebay.com/aw/announce.shtml

Check Account Status:
cgi3.ebay.aol.com/aw-cgi/eBayISAPI.dll?ViewAccountStatus

EBAY BOOKMARKS

Customer Support:
pages.ebay.aol.com/help/basics/select-support.html

Feedback Forum:
pages.ebay.com/services/forum/feedback.html

Fees:
pages.ebay.aol.com/help/sellerguide/selling-fees.html

Glossary of terms:
pages.ebay.com/help/basics/g-index.html

Help:
pages.ebay.com/help/index.html

How to Sell:
pages.ebay.aol.com/help/basics/n-selling.html

Photo Tutorial
pages.ebay.com/help/basics/phototut-1.html

Picture Services:
cgi4.ebay.aol.com/aw-cgi/eBayISAPI.dll?RegisterShow

Registration:
cgi4.ebay.aol.com/aw-cgi/eBayISAPI.dll?RegisterShow

Request Credit for eBay Commission:
pages.ebay.com/help/community/npb.html

Revise or update your auction information:
cgi5.ebay.aol.com/aw-cgi/eBayISAPI.dll?UserItemVerification

Search:
pages.ebay.com/search/items/search.html

Search by number:
pages.ebay.com/search/items/search_item.html

Search to find members:
cgi3.ebay.com/aw-cgi/eBayISAPI.dll?MemberSearchShow

Seller Services:
pages.ebay.aol.com/services/sellerservices.html

Shipping information:
pages.ebay.aol.com/services/buyandsell/shipping.html

Tips for Sellers:
pages.ebay.aol.com/help/sellerguide/selling-tips.html

To place or change your credit card information on eBay:
arribada.ebay.com/aw-secure/cc-update.html

HTML

As you learn to manipulate the HTML for your ads, you will find that you want to do more with the text and images. Here are some things you can do and the HTML for them:

HTML tutorial:
pages.ebay.aol.com/help/sellerguide/selling-html.html

Bold text: Your Text

Italic text: <i>Your Text</i>

Starts characters at next line:

Link to another website: <a href="URL">

Web Monkey:
hotwired.lycos.com/webmonkey/

Web Monkey for Kids (very simple HTML instructions):
hotwired.lycos.com/webmonkey/kids/lessons/web.html

Writing HTML lessons:
mcli.dist.maricopa.edu/tut/lessons.html

RESOURCES

AuctionRiches.com: Offers very helpful information and e-books, many of which are free. Highly recommended once you have mastered the basics.

Ask.com: One of the best information sources on any subject on the Internet

PayPal.com

manageauctions.com

BOOKS

Online Auctions @ eBay *by Dennis L Price*

eBay for Dummies *by Roland Woerner and others*

Digital Photography for Dummies *by Julie Adiar King*

The Official eBay Guide *by Era Fisher Kaiser and Michil Kaiser*

Starting an eBay Business for Dummies *by Marsha Collier*

Part of the reason I wrote about selling on eBay was that I had spent a great deal of time making all the mistakes possible on eBay, and I wanted to shorten the learning curve for other artists.

I spent a couple of hours each morning doing listings as well as follow-up on sales. There was no way to schedule auction starts on eBay at that time. I had to be at the computer at the best times to list. A good many hours went into my first $30,000 of earnings.

Don't sign up for every service offered or pursue every offer of "How to Make Millions on eBay." Whenever possible, use free services. Keep the auction description simple to save time when creating listings, especially at first.

With the evolution of eBay and the increased competition and number of listings in the art categories, my procedures have evolved also. After you have established your presence on eBay by using the techniques described in this chapter, you may decide to try my current strategy.

Recently, I've enlisted the help of an eBay Trading Assistant to do research and listings. The research is the kind of information that took so long to accumulate and put into this book. She creates and schedules my listings. My eBay time now—two or three hours a day—is spent pulling together the shipping information and handouts I send to each buyer as well as corresponding with eBay prospects and buyers. I depend on my Trading Assistant to correspond with buyers and bidders on common issues, but she forwards any question that she wants me to answer.

Consistent listings and reasonable prices are the two essentials for attracting buyers. In 2004, I have listed in two categories—Paintings/Contemporary and Self-Representing Artists—using Featured Auctions so that my work is in the beginning pages of the category listings. I start the auctions at $49 because more people will look and bid on a listing with a low starting bid. Bids attract more bids.

Within a few months of using this strategy, my ending bids have surpassed the bids at which most paintings sold initially. It was painful for a while, but it has been worth it. June 2004 was my best month to date.

CONCLUSION

Hopefully, the knowledge in this book will cut the eBay learning curve for you considerably.

The essential time management principle is to "keep it simple."

The more artworks you produce, the more you will sell.

Copyright Susan F Greaves

Still, it's a good idea to keep "lesser" work for the down times for which you don't expect high ending bids. Summer is usually slower, especially August. Sales reflect the ups and down of the economy. Right now, mine are booming!

I am on the verge of hiring someone to handle my records, paperwork, and shipping so that I can paint and produce even more to sell. One artist on eBay sells $30,000 per month and has about $6000 in expenses. That's a nice net! I've used a lot of her ideas, which she kindly shared with me, and now I've passed them to you.

Chapter 6

Designing Your Website

Design aspects

Sample site map

Creating images for the web

Meta tags

Security

Hiring a web master

Publishing your site

It don't mean a thing if it ain't got that swing.
Duke Ellington and Irving Mills

DESIGN ASPECTS

Creating your own site can be time-consuming, but it can also save you a lot of money.

Artist sites to browse:
- *silkspirit*
- *diegorivera*
- *douglass-truth*
- *marystreetart*
- *menloart*

Your aim as an artist showing artwork on the web, as with all your promotion, will be to use it as a portfolio.

It is important, whether you have the help of a web designer or not, that you have some basic knowledge. This chapter will inform you about basic site design.

This chapter is **not** meant to be a design manual but simply a guide to the general concepts of creating an art site. At the end of this chapter, you will find references to several books on web design. We suggest you study those if you will be designing your own site.

In the past, a designer had to know the HTML language in order to design a page. Since the Internet has become populated by the entire world, software programs have been developed and it's not necessary to know HTML. That makes it easier for small businessowners, like yourself, to design a site. Many web design programs exist: Macromedia Dreamweaver, Microsoft Front Page, Claris Home Page and more. Even professional designers use these programs.

An artist's website needs to be different from a commercial site such as www.amazon.com. You will need to show your particular "style" on your site.

TIPS

➤ Take a web design class. This will provide the training that you will need to familiarize yourself with a particular software design program. Make sure the class is being taught with a software design program that is compatible with your computer.

➤ Read some web design books (see end of chapter).

➤ Browse some sites on the Internet that have resources for building sites (see resources in Chapter 7).

➤ Decide on a specific style, theme, background color, etc.

➤ Design a site map (see page 89).

CHECK OUT OTHER SITES

➤ What background colors attract you?

➤ What types of layouts do you like?

➤ What features do you like about the pages you visited?

➤ How do their links work?

➤ What don't you like about these sites?

GUEST BOOKS

Give visitors the chance to leave their comments, e-mail address and home address so that you can contact them. Search for "free guest book" to download one for your site. Be sure to have a link from every page to your guest book, so a visitor can easily comment about your work.

404 ERRORS

Most likely, the software program you are using will have a built-in "link-checker" to verify that all your links are working. Should one of your links not work, a "404" error page will appear to the visitor.

You can customize your "404 error message" to say whatever you want. For instance, you can redirect the user back to your home page.

GENERAL DESIGN TIPS

➤ Keep your theme, logo and layout consistent.

➤ Use no more than two or three font families.

➤ Show products and services you will offer: originals, prints, other items.

➤ Identify the main purpose of your site.

Keep in mind that you have only eight seconds to keep the attention of your viewer. If your page doesn't pop up within eight seconds, you might lose your visitor.

Guest book sites:
* *guestpage*
* *recommend-it*

➤ Display your artwork no larger than 5x5" or so.

➤ Design a template, i.e., navigation bars, columns, tables, headers, logo.

➤ Have user-friendly navigation—for instance, phone and e-mail on each page.

➤ Make it possible for your visitor to go to any section on your site from any page; have all your site paths linked on each page: e-mail, order form, bio, statement, life story, prints, originals, etc.

➤ What will a client remember when he comes to your site to browse? Show your creative attitude through the design.

➤ Speed is an important design factor. Each page should download within 5-10 seconds. Test and check each page.

➤ List your prices! Label each work of art with the retail price. Why hide a good thing? People may think your artwork is too expensive if you don't inform them of the price.

➤ Exchanging links increases your search engine presence. Have a links page. Be innovative when exchanging links. Are you an environmental artist? Then find environment-related sites and ask them if they would like to exchange links. We recommend staying away from exchanging banners—just use word links. Too many banners on a page take too long to download and often create a sloppy impression.

➤ Keep your site simple. Too many bells and whistles are distracting.

➤ No blinking. Visitors did not come to your site to see how good a web designer you (or your web master) are; they came to see your artwork.

➤ No audio; your site is an art site, not a musical site.

➤ No advertisers; visitors have come to see your artwork and don't like distractions.

➤ Have your logo and/or name on every page.

➤ Type should be easy to read, not too small. Make sure the color of the type contrasts well with the background color.

➤ If you will be out of the office for a period of time, post a message on your home page indicating so. You don't want visitors to think that you don't answer e-mail.

➤ Display testimonials from people who have worked with you—consultants, galleries, buyers, etc.

➤ Be sure to list any sales you have made to well-known collectors on your bio page.

➤ Post any new items or events on your home page, with a link to a more detailed page. Otherwise, clients might not notice or find this new item.

➤ Include a casual picture of yourself, perhaps working at your easel. It helps people remember you.

➤ Post your life story, along with a well-composed bio and statement.

➤ If you are going to develop a newsletter, make past issues available to visitors in archives. Potential clients will like the fact that you have been developing as an artist over time.

➤ Splash pages are not necessary—just get to the point!

➤ Headings shouldn't overpower the design.

➤ Pick a theme, then design your page headers accordingly, or use your logo as headers.

➤ Ask yourself what viewers want to see when they arrive at your site. Provide that for them.

➤ Clarify your personal goal regarding the site. What do you want your visitors to know? What are your best assets?

➤ Remind your visitors to bookmark your home page.

➤ Solicit feedback from visitors through a survey, a question about how they select artwork to buy, etc. This can build traffic and provide e-mail addresses.

WEBSITE INNOVATION

• One artist created a great website with "Dorothy's Page." Dorothy is a fictional twin sister who confiscates this artist's work and sells it behind his back at a lower price. This idea got me to bookmark his site and go back there periodically to check on possible sale items.

• www.traceyporter.com has a link for "Dreamers and Entrepreneurs." This link caught my attention. I clicked on it right away.

Buying artwork online will become more and more accepted as time goes by. Presently, most people are hesitant to purchase an original online. Some ideas you can incorporate into your website to help them overcome this hesitancy include:

➤ 30-day approval

➤ money-back guarantee

➤ trade-ins

➤ payment installment plans

➤ framing service

➤ good customer service

➤ house visit (if possible)

Personalize your site. Try not to follow the pattern of typical, banner-inflated sites.

The biggest mistakes in artists' website design

- low-quality photos

- confusing navigation

- slow download

- animation, blinking, music

- links that don't work

- no prices listed

SAMPLE SITE MAP

Home

    ArtWork

        2003

        2002

        Abstracts

        Landscapes

    Prints

        Article such as *What is a giclée?*

        List of prints available

    Calendar

        Ongoing shows

        Upcoming shows

        Art shows of interest to the general public

        Cool art events around the U.S.

        Newsletter

    Reviews

        Magazine reviews

        Testimonials

    Links

        My favorite links

        Cool sites

        Helpful links

        Fun links

    Viewpoint

        Video reviews

        Book reviews

    History

        Bio

        Statement

        Life story

    Purchasing

        Shipping and handling policies

        Terms of purchase; guarantee

        Commissions

CREATING IMAGES FOR THE WEB

The most important part of displaying your artwork online is starting with a good photo. Digital cameras can be used for this purpose, but make sure to have lots of light when you take your photo—preferably natural light. Once you have a digital picture of your artwork, you will need to adapt it for the web by using a photo imaging program.

Photo imaging programs are fun to use but take a while to learn. Most graphic designers know how to use photo imaging software. You can create jpgs for online use with these programs.

All scanners (flatbed or slide) come with basic photo imaging programs that can size, rotate, colorize and twist images. This simple software is, most likely, all you will need to set up your site, providing your photography is done well. See Chapter 1.

TIPS

➤ Since small images are faster to download, give your viewers the option to choose which piece they want to see enlarged by listing a small thumbnail first. Large pieces should be no larger than 500 pixels in any direction. That way, the entire piece will be viewable at once on most monitors.

➤ A jpg's resolution should be at high-quality 72dpi. Make them the exact size you will be using on your page.

➤ www.ulead.com can help you optimize your images—that is, make them the most compact they can be. If you have many large images, or 30-plus small ones, on one page, you will need to do this.

➤ If you must make a choice, have your images be lighter rather than darker than the original.

➤ Break down web pages into sections so that they are not too long, with no more than 20 thumbnails on one page. Divide styles into two different pages—perhaps two genres, such as landscape and abstract.

➤ Jpgs must be created in RGB format, not CMYK (which is usually used for printing).

RESOURCES FOR PHOTO IMAGING SOFTWARE

➤ Adobe Photoshop is the most widely known imaging software program. If you use this sophisticated program, you'll probably need to take a class to understand its full benefits. Adobe also has a "consumer-grade" program that runs about $99.

➤ PaintShop is a less expensive program and quite sufficient for creating images for the web.

➤ You might find some photo software for free at www.shareware.com.

COPYRIGHTED IMAGES

All artwork is automatically copyrighted by the creator as it is being created. Although it breaks copyright laws and is punishable by law, an image on the Internet can be copied quite easily from your site to another. Most people are honest and do this only if they've asked for permission from the owner of the copyright. Unfortunately, there is not much you can do if someone steals an image of your artwork and posts it on their page without permission.

To protect yourself as much as possible, use 72dpi jpgs: Their printing quality is not high enough for commercial purposes. Your career most likely won't be ruined by somebody posting your image on their site at a lower resolution.

➤ If you find your artwork on another site, approach the site owner about it. They might not be knowledgable about your legal rights as creator and copyright owner.

➤ If you feel more comfortable doing so, you can actually incorporate your name in type right on the lower or upper part of any of your images before you put them online.

➤ Watermarking your jpgs is another possibility for protecting your work online, but it can be costly for individual artists.

Be sure to copyright your work in Washington, DC before you upload it onto the Internet. See our book Art Marketing 101 for detailed information.

META TAGS

Once you have the visual portion of your site designed, you will want to dedicate a lot of time to designing the "interior."

Hidden from view within every page on the Internet is a group of "meta tags"—keywords, description and title—hidden to the naked eye but visible to search engines. Search engines use these meta tags to categorize your site.

KEYWORDS

A great site where you can create meta tags and keyword groupings that will best promote your site for free is wordtracker.com/ third party/addme

Keywords are what search engines use to find and list your site. When thinking of keywords to use to promote your work, try to think the way someone searching for your type of art would think. A collector might be interested in vibrant colors, abstract expressionism, living artist, price range, etc. These words are what you want to list in your keyword section.

Find out what other artists are using for their keywords. When on their site, click "View" on the navigator bar, then go to "Page Source." You will be able to see keywords they use on any page!

TIPS

➤ Many search engines detect if you are using more than 25 key-words on any given page, and they tend not to respond well to more than 25.

➤ Because the word "painting" is so generic (as well as gallery, artwork, artist), a search done using just the word "painting" will pull up millions of sites. Use words that are not generic—for example, spiritual art, shamanic art, three-dimensional painting, earth works, sublime art, sculptural ceramics, etc.).

Repeat important words in all the three sections— keywords, description and title.

➤ Don't repeat words in the keyword section. You can have varia-tions on each word, such as art, artist, artists, arts, artworld, art-work, etc . . . but do not put artist, artist, artist.

➤ When using a phrase like "commissioned portraits" the keywords could read: commission, commissioned portrait, portrait.

➤ Separate keywords by commas. No spaces are necessary.

➤ Have your first and last name together as well as separate: ivo david, ivo, david.

➤ Put all keywords in lowercase.

WHAT THE HIDDEN CODE LOOKS LIKE ON A SITE

```
<HTML>

<HEAD>

  <META NAME="GENERATOR" CONTENT="Adobe PageMill">

  <META NAME="keywords" CONTENT=" ivo david, ivo, david, oil painting,
oils, painting, acrylic, collage, new age, two-dimensional, oil on canvas, artwork,
fusionism">

  <META NAME="description" CONTENT="Gallery carrying two-dimensional
artwork of ivo david, including oil, acrylic and collage">

  <TITLE>Ivo David </title>

</HEAD>
```

KEYWORD SECTION

DESCRIPTION SECTION

PAGE TITLE SECTION

Keyword resources:
- *overture.com*
- *wordtracker.com*

DESCRIPTIONS

In the description section of your meta tags, you will be writing, in sentence format, a summary of your site. Pull out some words from your keyword section and use those in your description. You can have several sentences within the description. This description is what comes up when someone does a search (see below).

TITLES

Be very specific with the title on each of your pages. The title plays an important role in the process that determines where your page shows up on a search engine. The title page is the first thing the spider of a search engine looks at. A title should be helpful to visitors, but also useful to search engines. Use no more than five words; the shorter and more concise, the better the search engines respond.

SECURITY

A secured site is necessary when selling a quantity of items (books, prints, mugs, magnets, etc.) at low prices ($1 - 99). For a fine artist selling original artwork, a secured site is not necessary. Potential clients of original artwork (ranging from $250 and up) will normally want to talk to the artist before purchasing. In fact, it's better, if you're selling only originals, to have the potential client call you. That way you will have more personal contact and will be able to help them better—perhaps even sell them more. Remember, an artist needs to have personal contact with his customers. There is no substitute for a one-to-one meeting or phone conversation with a purchaser.

A client may want to pay with a credit card. If you are already set up to accept credit cards off-line, take her credit card number over the phone and process it. If you are not set up in this manner, perhaps you want to use one of the secured paying services to accommodate your client's needs. Alternatively, you can accept a standard check.

SECURED PAYMENT SERVICES

These companies take your customer's credit card number, secure the appropriate funds while you send your customer the goods, then pay you the money when the customer has received and approved (usually in 5-10 days) the product. They have electronic transfer and credit-card encryption programs to protect your clients.

PayPal - Three types of accounts are available: **Personal**, limited to $100 in purchases per month in credit card payments, no fee; **Premier**, more than $100 in purchases per month, 30¢ fee + 2.2%; and **Business**, intended for business use only (you're a business!). With this option, you can accept payment through your website and use PayPal's shopping cart, 30¢ fee + 2.9%.

BidPay - A Western Union subsidiary, they send you a money order for purchases going through them. Limit: $700. Fee: $5 + 2.25%.

PayDirect - From Yahoo. No fees for a personal account. Minimum amount of money you can spend is $5; maximum $200.

C2IT - Citibank-sponsored. Fees depend on type of transaction, from 1% to 1.6%.

SHOPPING CARTS

Shopping carts cost a fair amount to set up, but they have a real advantage if you have the appropriate items to sell.

For an individual artist, a shopping cart is not needed unless you are selling prints, magnets, cups, cards, etc. If you think you need to have a shopping cart on your site:

➤ go to www.shoppingcarts.com

➤ go to an "online site builder" such as www.monstercommerce.com, a shopping cart system to which you can subscribe, often costing only $5 per month.

HIRING A WEB MASTER

Remember: This is your site, not a site for a web master to show off his super-techno abilities.

Unless you can dedicate a lot of time to learning a new software program, it's best to think about hiring a web designer to create your site (or publish with an online gallery).

If you hire a designer, you should not leave choices entirely up to him. Get involved with the design or you might be sorry later. And remember, some web masters are not web designers. Look at some sites she has created before you commit to work with her.

Browse the Internet. Print out pages you like, as well as ones you don't like. Note colors you find pleasant. Have as much information together for your designer as possible.

Did you know: When you hire a web designer to build your site, it becomes the copyrightable artwork of the designer, just as when you create a commission for someone, it is your copyrighted image, not the buyer's. If you want to change or update the site yourself in the future, or hire a different person to update it, you cannot! The only way to avoid this inconvenience is to have a written agreement with the web master indicating that you own all the rights to her creation and that you can change it as needed. If the web master doesn't agree to that, find a different one! Since updating with a designer costs a mint, you'll probably want to learn to update your site yourself.

WEB MASTER CONTRACTS SHOULD INCLUDE:

➤ Agreement on the copyright ownership issue

➤ Cost of initial development and what it includes

➤ Cost for updates after initial development

➤ Rights to keep a copy of your site on your computer

➤ A web master lays out the visuals. Find out if she also knows how to design the hidden parts of pages—how to put in meta tags so you will get the best possible listings with search engines.

WEB DESIGNERS

Web designers generally charge $25-50 per hour. If they are in high demand and busy, be prepared to pay $75-plus an hour! Just the fact that they charge a lot doesn't mean they are fast. You should be able to get a comprehensive quote, especially if you have read this chapter and have outlined a preliminary version of your site. The minimum price I have seen for a home page design for an artist is about $375. That includes only one to five pages of design. Most sites cost a minimum $1000. Depending on how many updates you plan to do during the year, you should estimate a minimum of $300-500 per year for future updates. In addition to your web design fee, you will have an annual URL registration fee (about $15-25) and monthly ISP fees (about $10-25).

The best way to choose a web designer is to surf to a website you like and see who designed it—usually their e-mail and name are at the bottom of the first page. We list here a few designers who have experience working with artists' sites.

WEB DESIGNERS

Jason Kurst
530.559.6842   <jason@badboywebdesign.com>
www.badboywebdesign.com
Specializes in gallery and artist sites. He also helped edit this book.

Kurt Irmiter
828.658.2779 <kurt@festivalnet.com>   www.festivalnet.com
He is ArtNetwork's ISP host and helped us design a few of our CGI pages. He is customer service-oriented, which makes a big difference in efficiency.

Darryl Rubarth
775.884.0699 www.zartist.com

Gabriel Jeffrey
617.395.6646 <gabe@uigui.com>   www.uigui.com
Specializes in sites for the arts—fine artists, musicians and more. Proficient in user-interface.

TESTING YOUR SITE

Once your site is designed, you will need to upload, or publish, it onto the Internet. You will need a File Transfer Protocol/FTP software program to upload your site's pages onto the WWW. Most of the more sophisticated site-design software programs have upload programs built into them. If you've hired a designer, he will do this for you.

➤ Netscape Communicator comes with an FTP program called Publish. You can download it from www.netscape.com/download.

➤ One of the most commonly used programs to upload onto the Internet is Fetch.

➤ Interarchy is another program available.

➤ WS FTP LE (a PC-friendly FTP program) is free and easy to use. Download it from www.tucows.com.

➤ Another PC-friendly program is CuteFTP from www.globalscape.com.

After you've uploaded your site to the Internet, you will need to make sure it looks good, works well, and links and prints out correctly.

➤ Compatibility. Test your site on a "foreign" computer—your friend's, a local Internet cafe, the library, etc. It might appear differently on all those computers. Make sure you try it on both a Mac and a PC. You can also check how fast it downloads on each one.

➤ Check for spelling and grammar errors.

➤ Check for color scheme, layout and visual balance.

➤ Double-check all the links.

➤ Have several people, both friends and business associates, review the site before you advertise it to the world. See what they say. Do they find it user-friendly?

➤ When all looks and works well, you are ready to let everyone know you are up and running.

www.optiview.com is a site that helps fine-tune sites by checking the download time. It estimates how a shorter download time can be achieved by editing images for free.

TRACKING BROKEN LINKS ONLINE

www.netmechanic.com will check your links, page-load time and spelling for about $60 per 100 pages. Some other sites where you can check your links:

anybrowser   hitbox   linkalarm   linkbot

TIPS

➤ Don't use strange characters in your file names, such as #, ?, *, etc. They can create errors when uploading to some sites.

➤ If you don't have the correct suffix (.html, .jpg) in a file name, it won't be recognized by the World Wide Web and will not link properly.

❑ Search other artists' sites for ideas. Print out the pages you like.

❑ Decide what products and services your website will offer.

❑ Identify the main purpose of your website: What do you want to say about your artwork?

❑ Decide on an approach to your site: formal, casual, whimsical, etc.

❑ List three things you want your visitor to do at your site.

❑ Design a site map.

❑ Write keywords, title and description for your main page.

❑ Draw a rough layout of your site's design on paper.

❑ Decide whether to build your site, hire a web designer or use an online gallery.

RECOMMENDED READING

Creating Web Pages for Dummies *by Bud E Smith*

Design Your Own Home Page *by Molly E Holzschlag*

Designing Web Usability: The Practice of Simplicity *by Jakob Nielsen*

Digital Photography for Dummies *by Julie Adiar King*

Don't Make Me Think: A Common Sense Approach to Web Usability *by Steve Krug and Roger Black*

Electronic Highway Robbery *by Mary E Carter*

Home Page Usability: 50 Websites Deconstructed *by Jakob Nielsen*

How to Design and Build the Coolest Website in Cyberspace *by Jerry Glenwright*

User-Centered Web Design *by John Cato*

Web Content Management: A Collaborative Approach *by Russell Nakano*

ACTION PLAN

_____

_____

_____

_____

_____

_____

_____

_____

Chapter 7
Making a Splash on the Web

Promotional prep

Links

Guerrilla tactics

Getting return visitors

PDF files

Search engines

Press lists

Tracking visitors

You must do the thing you think you cannot do. Eleanor Roosevelt

PROMOTIONAL PREP

In this chapter, you'll be shown a variety of ways to get quality visitors to your site. You've spent lots of money and effort to get your artwork online. Don't blow your investment! Energy spent promoting your site is the only way you'll get potential clients to view it.

As a fine artist you will not be thinking of promotion in the same way a large company does. You need to think of attracting individual, quality clients. Concentrate on certain key art professionals such as interior designers, corporate art consultants, architects, private collectors, publishers, licensors, etc. Why would they be searching for you? Did they see your work at a gallery or show? Did you give them your business card at an exhibition?

PROMOTION SERVICES

For a fee, these services will assist you with different parts of your promotion. If you don't have the time, these services can fit the bill. You can do many of the promotions yourself for free.

activemarketplace	affordable-website-promotion
bob-baker	chrismaher
deadlock	freewebware
goodkeywords	ineedhits
isubmit	jimtools
keywordranking	marketingtips
positionagent	selfpromotion
submitplus	virtualpromote
website-submission	websitepublicity
wildlife-fantasy	wilsonweb

LINKS

The general idea is to create as many paths to your site as possible. Reciprocal links are one way to do just that. Linking your site to a site that is associated in some way with your artwork is one of the best ways to drive potential customers to your pages.

To know what sites you might want to trade (or exchange) links with, think about what sites your potential clients might be browsing. If you do floral paintings, perhaps clients interested in nature-type paintings might browse to gardens, nurseries, flower arrangers and flower sites. Check out these sites by doing a search. Then ask each site individually if you can exchange links.

➤ If you've written an article, perhaps they would want to feature it on their site. Many site editors are looking for content, so don't be shy if you have a good article to submit.

➤ You could also offer the use of one of your floral art images on their site.

Art galleries, art organizations (especially your local art council) and art publications are all sites to which you need to be linked.

RECIPROCAL LINK SOFTWARE

You can find out who is linking to your site by going to:

linkpopularitycheck   cyber-robotics   links4trade

AFFILIATE PROGRAMS/BANNER ADS

Once your site is up, companies may approach you by e-mail to ask you to participate in their affiliate programs, which usually means placing their banner ad on your site. They will offer money. Don't do this. Display only your own artwork. Don't clutter your site.

TIP

➤ Too many banners on one page take too much time to download and often look chaotic. Simply list the link name, with no banner, and perhaps with a short written description.

Broadcasts and chatrooms (already discussed in Chapters 2 and 3) are two other tactics to promote your URL.

WEB RINGS

Web rings are a way to have viewers with a common interest find sites covering this subject. For instance, if you are an equine artist, you might want to join a web ring for horse enthusiasts. Since each person's site in the ring is linked to the next, you can visit hundreds of sites on the same topic (and possibly exchange links).

ringsurf   webring.org

PAY-PER-CLICK

The purpose of a pay-per-click account is to have your site listed at the top of a search engine. Generally a "click" costs 5-10¢.

At Google, one of the best search engines to get "ad-words," you can limit your budget to any amount per month. Google will stop listing you after you have arrived at that budgeted amount. Google explains all their policies online at www.google.com.

CONTESTS

The main idea of having a contest is to gather new names, new potential clients. Make it a requirement that a participant leave her e-mail as well as her snail mail address so that you can promote to her in the future. You might require her to answer a few questions about her art interests—for example does she collect a particular style of art? Make it clear to the surfer that you will not sell his info—it is for your use only.

➤ www.contestsguide.com is a site full of contests. Studying them will help you figure out your own strategy for holding one.

➤ You can let people who have previously visited your site find out about your contest via a broadcast.

➤ www.webmagnet.com will expose you to the best contests on the web. Mimic their promotion. They have a great page of general promotion advice, too.

➤ Have a title contest for one of your new artworks and give away a print of it. Perhaps holding the contest on a monthly basis will bring clients back.

TEASERS

Post something on your home page to entice visitors to come back.

➤ Going to interview a famous artist soon? Note that on your home page so people will bookmark and come back to read your interview.

GUERRILLA TACTICS

➤ Going to write about a particular topic next quarter? Ask visitors what they would like to learn about.

GIFT CERTIFICATES

Offer an online gift certificate, which your patrons can purchase for a friend. Send it to them via e-mail or snail mail. Create a system of numbering your certificates, and be sure to keep track of them on a sheet in your office. If two certificates come in with the same number, you should be alerted that something strange is going on.

ARTICLES

Write an article that will attract art collectors to your site. Focus your marketing efforts on getting various sites to carry these articles. Your articles' titles may sound like these:

➤ 7 Steps to Enjoying Your Purchased Artwork

➤ Suggestions for Displaying Your Artwork

➤ Developing a Sculpture Garden

For example, if you are an abstract painter, write an article about your philosophy on viewing abstract art. Submit it to a site—architectural magazine, interior designer, etc.—and see if they would like to use it. If they post the article, make sure there is a link to your site attached to it.

ARTICLE SUBMISSIONS

ArtAffairs   absolutearts

govt.ucsd.edu/newjour/submit   published.com/add

newsletteraccess.com/database/reg.html

GETTING RETURN VISITORS

Why would someone want to return to your site? You need to answer this question! A return visitor indicates a lot of interest. Here are a few strategies:

➤ Update your site monthly with interesting information.

➤ Review videos you've seen, using your original artistic style.

➤ Write an artistic critique on particular art books.

➤ Every month, offer a special price on one original piece: first come, first served. Let it be known on your entry page that you do this. Perhaps have a monthly auction. Do something consistently and people will come back.

➤ If you auction on eBay, let visitors coming to your site know this fact.

➤ Offer something free.

➤ E-mail former visitors informing them of the completion of an art piece.

➤ Ask visitors for an opinion: Do you prefer artwork #1 or artwork #2?

➤ Having a calendar of events on your site can bring people back. You can download calendars: www.mattkruse.com or www.cgi-world.com/calendar.html.

TIP

➤ www.internet-tips.net has articles about how to improve your Internet savvy.

PDF FILES

This book has reached you as a file called a Portable Document Format/PDF file. PDF files can be read on any type of computer that has Acrobat Reader software. Acrobat Reader is downloadable for free from www.adobe.com.

You can attach a PDF document (for example, one of your articles) to an e-mail and broadcast to your entire address book, or you can upload a PDF document to your website. Visitors can then download it.

CREATING A PDF FILE

To create a PDF file, you will need a software program called Acrobat Distiller ($250). Directions on creating a PDF document are simple and come with the manual.

Adobe, creator of Acrobat products, has an online PDF creator that can be accessed through their website, www.adobe.com. You plug in your file and select the options you want. It creates the PDF document. You will get your first five documents for free. After that, you pay only $9.95 for a month of unlimited PDFs.

SEARCH ENGINES

Ninety-eight percent of all searches made online use five main search engines: Google, Yahoo, MSN, Alta Vista and Ask. To list your site with these main search engines, you will only need to go to two places:

➤ www.dmoz.org - When you submit your information to this site, all the other search engines will pick it up.

➤ www.yahoo.com

ART DIRECTORIES

An art directory is a search engine with art-related topics, including names of artists. This is where you want to be listed. Below is a list of not-to-be-missed art directories in which to list your URL.

DATABASES

artincontext.org	artline	artareas
dart.fine-art	fineartexplorer.com	wwar

Many arts councils have their own directories online. Join and support your local organization. It is the most common place a person searches for a local artist to commission a mural or portrait.

Remember, for a visual artist, quantity of visitors is not the point: Quality of visitors is more important.

III

PRESS LISTS

Until you are working on a very special art project, stick with the previously mentioned promotions. Press releases need to present a very unusual project in order to get placed in a publication, off- or online—for example, artist sculpts figures from ice, artist helps raise $20,000 for animal shelter.

Sending out thousands of spams to an e-mail press list doesn't work if you don't have the right project to atract attention. When you do have that original art project, contact one of the companies on the list below to help you get press coverage.

Internetwire.com - For $79, your press release will be distributed to over 9000 media outlets internationally. Mostly, companies with well-known (or avant garde new products) use this service.

PRNewsire.com - Subscribe to their free online newsletter to see what other artists might be doing.

gopressrelease	mypressrelease	uniqueseek
xpresspress	prweb	

Have a tracking system to see how many people have visited your website, and whence they came. By reading these reports (which can, at first, seem as foreign as your first financial statement), you will be able to modify your design, meta tags and keywords to get positioned correctly for the best traffic to your site.

You can even find out which of your web pages a visitor came to first (and maybe think about improving that popular page) or what search engine they used. Make sure that your ISP host can track visitors in the above manner.

You will want to find out:

➤ Number of hits per page

➤ Number of visitors per day

➤ What pages are the most visited on your site

➤ What links are not linking properly (i.e., a 404 error message occurs)

➤ Where the visitors are coming from: a reciprocal link, a search engine, etc.

STATISTICS GENERATORS

If your ISP doesn't have a stat page, use one of the following sites:

counted   pagetools.com/cyberstats/admin2.html

freestats   nedstat.net

HOW WELL HAVE YOU PROMOTED YOUR SITE?

Ranking is the placement of your URL on the search engines.

➤ www.rankings.com is an online tool to help you determine your search engine ranking.

➤ www.rankthis.com will do a free check of your site's ranking in several of the main search engines.

➤ www.positionagent.com will track where the top 10 search engines and directories rank you. You pay for six months of service and submit URL/keyword pairs for the service to monitor. Using this information, you will get reports on where you rank. You will receive weekly e-mail reports detailing your page and position ranking.

TRACKING VISITORS

Tracking Your Website Visitors by Chris Maher can be accessed at *www.1x.comadvisor/ maher12.htm*

Promote your site off-line —via postcards, telephone calls, invites—to former (or existing) clients.

ACTION PLAN

❑ Make a list of appropriate sites and ask them to reciprocate links.

❑ Search for some web rings that suit your genre of art.

❑ Develop a strategy that will bring visitors back.

❑ Write an article for use on other sites.

❑ Learn how to create a PDF file.

❑ Submit your site to dmoz.org.

❑ Learn to read your stat report.

❑ Find out where you rank in the search engines.

RECOMMENDED READING

101 Ways to Boost Your Web Traffic *by Thomas Wong*

Branding Yourself Online *by Bob Baker*

Getting Hits: The Definitive Guide to Promoting Your Website *by Don Sellers*

Guerrilla Marketing Online Weapons: 100 Low-Cost, High-Impact Weapons for Online Profits and Prosperity *by Jay Conrad Levison*

Increase Your Web Traffic in a Weekend *by William Robert Stanek*

Increasing Hits and Selling More on Your Website *by Greg Helmstetter*

The Internet Publicity Guide: How to Maximize Your Marketing and Promotion in Cyberspace *by V A Shiva*

Internet Publicity Resources *by Steve O'Keefe*

Maximize Website Traffic *by Robin Nobles and Susan O'Neil*

Planning Your Internet Marketing Strategy *by Ralph E Wilson*

Website Stats: Tracking Hits and Analyzing Web Traffic *by Rick Stout*

Chapter 8
Search and You Shall Find

Sites to browse

Do what you can, with what you have, right where you are.
Theodore Roosevelt

SITES TO BROWSE

There are so many sites, thousands of new ones monthly, that it's impossible to compile a complete listing. It's best to go online and do a search for what you need. We'll give you a start here, however, in a few different categories. You can also go online to our site at www.artmarketing.com/links and access about 20 various topics of links.

ACCOUNTING SITES

irs.gov

smartmoney

cbs.marketwatch

taxguide.completetax

APPRAISERS

appraiseitnet

appraisers

appraisersassoc.org

artworth

collectingchannel

ART NEWS

artforum

artnet

wwar

BARTERING

ctebarter

intagio

itex

microtechsys

COMPETITIONS FOR ARTISTS

artdeadlines

artmarketing.com/hotline

COPYRIGHT FORMS

loc.gov/copyright/circs

FINE ART REPRODUCTIONS

art

artrepublic

artseek

barewalls

beyond the wall

corbis

FUNDING AND GRANTS

fdncenter.org

arts.endow.gov

moneyforart

nasaa-arts.org

GALLERIES

artcanyon

art4business

collectfineart

fineartsite

galleryonline

image4is

itheo

justoriginals

- latinarte
- nextmonet
- neoimages
- paintingsdirect
- photocollect
- visualize

INSURANCE

- fineartguy
- chubb

MAGAZINES

- artnewsonline
- sunshineartist
- shawguides

MATERIALS

- dickblick
- sinopia
- whslartframe
- aaronbrothers
- 1000sofdiscountbooks
- discountart

MISCELLANEOUS SITES

arts4allpeople.org -The Wallace Reader's Digest Fund and an advisory board of arts leaders and funding partners have developed a website for individuals and organizations committed to promoting new ideas and practices in the arts. The site features success stories, an online library of practical research, resources and discussion boards.

jimmott - Jim has been traveling around the country painting and selling his art. He has a unique and interesting tale.

rejectioncollection - The artist's online source for misery, commiseration and rejection letters

streetstudio - A pair of innovative photographers walk the streets of New York City (they started long before 9/11) with the intent of photographing every person in the city of eight million. So far they are up to 20,000.

superpages.com/yp4.superpages.com - Search an area within a 5- to100-mile radius for businesses: galleries, architects, interior designers, frame shops, etc.

usps.com/ncsc/lookups/lookup_zip+4.html - A quick and easy way to look up zip codes

ORGANIZATIONS

artbusiness

artdealers.org

artswire.org

artistresource.org

cityofseattle.net/arts

fada

fota

sculptor.org

watercolor-online

ylem.org

POLITICAL ACTION

artsusa.org

PURCHASING COMPUTER ACCESSORIES

outpost

pricewatch

RESEARCH

artlex

SCHOOLS

artbusinessacademy

artmarketingworkshops

masterclassstudios

SCULPTURE

artnut

SHIPPING SERVICES

fedex

fineartship

ups

usps

TRADE SHOWS

artmethods

artexpos

surtex

Bold type = Businesses   *Italic type = Books*

INDEX

Bold type = Businesses   *Italic type = Books*

INDEX

Bold type = Businesses   *Italic type = Books*

Mailing Lists

		PRICE PER LIST
1.	47,000 Visual Artists	$100 per 1000
2.	900 Art Councils	$80
3.	350 Art Publications	$50
4.	1700 Art Publishers	$150
4A.	900 Greeting Card Publishers	$75
4B.	130 Print Distributors	$50
4C.	350 Greeting Card Sales Reps	$50
4D.	225 Licensing Contacts	$50
4E.	180 Calendar Publishers	$50
5.	400 Book Publishers	$50
6.	535 Corporations Collecting Art	$60
6A.	160 Corporations Collecting Photography	$50
7.	750 Art Stores	$65
8.	1950 Reps, Consultants, Brokers, Dealers	$150
8A.	170 Corporate Art Consultants	$50
9.	1900 College Art Departments	$150
9A.	1900 College Galleries	$150
10.	600 Libraries	$60
11.	6500 Galleries	$80 per 1000
11A.	425 Photo Galleries	$50
11B.	800 New York City Galleries	$70
11C.	1300 California Galleries	$95
12.	550 Foreign Galleries	$70
12B.	250 Canadian Galleries	$50
13.	2500 Art Organizations and Exhibition Spaces	$170
13A.	450 Art Organization Newsletters	$60
14.	1000 Art Museums	$75
14A.	625 Art Museum Gift Store Buyers	$75
15.	800 Architects	$70
16.	700 Interior Designers	$65
17.	1900 Frame and Poster Galleries	$150

All lists can be rented for onetime use and may not be copied, duplicated or reproduced in any form. Lists have been seeded to detect unauthorized usage. Reorder of same lists within a 12-month period qualifies for 25% discount. Lists cannot be returned or exchanged.

FORMATS/CODING
All domestic names are provided in zip code sequence on three-up pressure-sensitive labels. We mail to each company/person on our list a minimum of once per year. Our business thrives on responses to our mailings, so we keep them as up-to-date and clean as we possibly can.

SHIPPING
Please allow one week for processing your order once your payment has been received. Lists are sent Priority Mail and take an additional 2-4 days. Orders sent without shipping costs will be delayed. $5 shipping per order.

GUARANTEE
Each list is guaranteed 95% deliverable. We will refund 37¢ per piece for undeliverable mail in excess of 5% if returned to us within 90 days of order.

ArtNetwork
530·470·0862   800·383·0677   530·470·0256 Fax
PO Box 1360, Nevada City, CA 95959-1360
www.artmarketing.com   <info@artmarketing.com>

Books

Learn how to gain exposure as a fine artist. Read about myths many artists fall prey to and how to avoid them. Identify roadblocks to success. You'll learn about:

* **Preparing a portfolio** * **Pricing your work** * **Secrets of successful artists**
* **Alternative venues for selling** * **Legal matters** * **Succeeding without a rep**
* **Developing a marketing plan** * **Publicity**

Learn what art schools don't teach: **business savvy**. No other book offers artists such concise step-by-step marketing strategies. This book answers such questions as:

* Must I depend on dealers, curators and gallery owners—or can I do it on my own?
* How do I protect my work from plagiarism?

This comprehensive 24-chapter volume covers all the key issues any artist needs to know to do business in today's world and includes:

* Case histories and success stories
* Checklists to help you stay on track
* "Action Plan" at the end of each chapter

$24.95 **336 pages** **ISBN: 0-940899-32-9** **2003 edition** **$4 shipping**

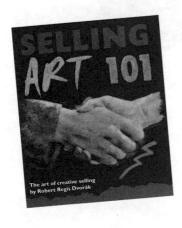

This book is for artists, reps and galleries. The art of selling art needs to be learned. This book provides easy-to-approach techniques that will save years of frustration. The right attitude, combined with the information in this book, will take your career to new levels. Robert Dvorák has been teaching artists, art representatives and art gallery sales personnel powerful and effective selling methods for over 24 years. He has sold his own work in the USA, Europe, Japan, China, and Indonesia to individual collectors and corporate clients. This book will teach you how to:

* **Develop rapport with clients**
* **How to get referrals**
* **About tie-downs**
* **Telephone techniques**
* **Closing secrets**
* **14 power words**

* **Studio selling**
* **How to use emotions**
* **Listening techniques**
* **Overcoming objections**
* **Goal setting**

$22.95 **192 pages** **ISBN: 0-940899-86-8** **2004 edition** **$4 shipping**

Living Artists

In this competitive and fast-paced world, an artist needs to take marketing seriously. Here's a way to do it dynamically and economically! *Living Artists* (formerly titled the *Encyclopedia of Living Artists*) is a direct link to prime customers—including reps, corporate art consultants, gallery owners, interior designers , museum curators and more. These artworld professionals use this book to select artwork throughout the year for various projects. Artwork in the book is reproduced in high-quality full-color, along with artist's name, address and telephone number. Prospective buyers have direct contact with the artist of choice. All fine artists are invited to submit their work. Published biannually in odd-numbered years. A contest is conducted for the cover position. For a prospectus (August 2004 and 2006 deadlines), e-mail to info@artmarketing.com.

ArtNetwork
530·470·0862   800·383·0677   530·470·0256 Fax
PO Box 1360, Nevada City, CA 95959-1360
www.artmarketing.com   <info@artmarketing.com>

More Books

Business Forms, Charts, Sample Letters, Legal Documents, Business Plans

This book provides artists with a wide selection of indispensable business forms, charts, sample letters, legal documents and business plans . . . all for photocopying. Organize your office's administrative and planning functions. Reduce routine paperwork and increase time for your art creation. 80+ forms

80+ forms include:

12-month planning calendar ❧ Sales agreement
Model release ❧ Rental-lease agreement ❧ Form VA
Slide reference sheet ❧ Competition record
Customer-client record ❧ Phone-zone sheet
Monthly project status form ❧ Marketing plan
12-month show planner ❧ Checklist for a juried show
Print planning calendar ❧ Bill of sale
Pricing worksheet ❧ Press release ❧ and lots more

$16.95   112 pages   ISBN: 0-940899-27-2   2003 edition $4 shipping
Also available in PDF format for $14.95 (no shipping costs)

Publishing and Licensing Your Artwork for Profit

Learn how to increase your income by licensing your art. Reaching this industry takes special knowledge. That's exactly what you'll receive in this book: assistance from an expert. The first part of the book has information about conducting business with the publishing and licensing industry; the second part lists contacts in the industry with names, addresses, telephone numbers, web sites and what type of art the company is looking for. Includes 200 listings of licensing companies, publishers and more.

You'll learn about:

✳ **Negotiating fees**
✳ **How to approach various markets**
✳ **Targeting your presentation**
✳ **Trade shows**
✳ **Licensing agents**
✳ **Protecting your rights**
✳ **Self-publishing**

Over 200 listings:

☞ **Calendar publishers**
☞ **Licensing agents**
☞ **Greeting card publishers**
☞ **Print and poster publishers**

$23.95   256 pages   ISBN:0-940899-77-2   2003 edition $4 shipping

www.artmarketing.com/gallery

Your web page with ArtNetwork will include five reproductions of your artwork (example below). Each artwork clicks onto an enlarged rendition, approximately three times the size. Two hundred words of copy (whatever you want to say) are allowed.

Our site averages 700 visitors a day (and going up each quarter), with the gallery being the second most visited area on our site (the first is our main page).

▲ Your home page on our site will be seen by important members of the art world. We publicize our site to art publishers, gallery owners, museum curators, consultants, architects, interior designers and more! We receive over 225,000 hits per month.

▲ You will have an address that will take your customers directly to your artwork. Your address will have your name in it, i.e., www.artmarketing.com/gallery/johndoe.

▲ You will want to put this web address on business cards, letterhead, envelopes, brochures, flyers, and any advertising you do. Tell the world where you live on the Internet so they will come see what you do!

$220 FOR 2 YEARS

To showcase your artwork on-line send:

- Five images for ArtNetwork to scan; a combination of horizontal and vertical is fine. You can send photo prints/35mm slides/jpgs. Note on slides "top front." If you send a photo/print, it can be no smaller than 2x2 ", no larger than 8x10 ". Artwork is electronically scanned and reproduced, using 72 dpi resolution. No color corrections are made, so send well-taken pieces or jpgs.
- A list of the five images: title, size, medium, retail price, and if prints are available, cost and size of prints.
- Check, money order or charge card number (VISA/MC/AmExpress/Discover): $220 for two years of service.
- Legible copy of no more than 200 words.
- E-mail address
- A #10 SASE for return of your materials